PENGUIN BOOKS

WHAT IS DUNGEONS AND DRAGONS?

Dungeons and Dragons is the fastest-growing game in the Western world. Every year, thousands of people join this fascinating hobby. Since its release in 1974, it has proved to be one of the most popular games ever made.

Philip Parker, John Butterfield and David Honigmann are well-qualified to write a book on Dungeons and Dragons as they have been playing it since 1977 and have recently set up a club at their school, Eton College, to teach and play the game.

John was born in 1965. His interests include football, jogging and bridge. Philip, born in the same year, enjoys playing chess and reading science-fiction and fantasy literature. David is a year younger, and is interested in computers, debating and reading *anything*.

WHAT IS

Dungeons and Dragons?

✠

JOHN BUTTERFIELD

DAVID HONIGMANN

PHILIP PARKER

PENGUIN BOOKS

Penguin Books Ltd, Harmondsworth, Middlesex, England
Penguin Books, 625 Madison Avenue, New York, New York 10022, U.S.A.
Penguin Books Australia Ltd, Ringwood, Victoria, Australia
Penguin Books Canada Ltd, 2801 John Street, Markham, Ontario, Canada LR3 1B4
Penguin Books (N.Z.) Ltd, 182–190 Wairau Road, Auckland 10, New Zealand

—

First published 1982

—

Made and printed in Great Britain by
Hazell Watson & Viney Ltd, Aylesbury, Bucks
Set in Sabon by Rowland Phototypesetting Ltd
Bury St Edmunds, Suffolk

✢ Contents ✢

✠ Introduction ✠

Slammer Kyntire is a fighter. Some days ago, together with a few friends, he was searching for the Sword of the Sorcerer in the ruins of the ancient shrine of Kollchap when he was surprised by a band of hobgoblins. The adventurers managed to escape, cutting down two of the creatures, but in the ensuing pursuit Slammer's arm was hit by a crossbow bolt. Back at an inn, Zhod the priest heals the injured limb while secretly the fighter plots for the day when he can buy back his father's farm from the landlord who has seized it and enslaved his family.

Hotfa Nap is a sorceress from one of the nomad tribes of the Mesta Desert. Unfairly accused of witchcraft, she slipped away at night and travelled to join the College of Magicians under Dokhon. She has a violent aversion to the necromancers of the rival College of Khan and their servants of living stone, the rockmen.

Gripper 'the Skin' Longshank was born into a border tribe of the Albine empire. Moving south into the empire with some other members of his tribe to visit the big cities, he was seduced into crime by two professional thieves who turned a handy profit out of his talents as a pickpocket before he was arrested and abandoned by them. On his release, he vowed to track down his two patrons and be revenged on them; he would willingly sacrifice anyone to achieve this, even his two fellow-adventurers, Slammer and Hotfa.

These, however, are no flesh-and-blood characters. They exist only as a collection of numbers on several sheets of paper, as little metal figures, and, most importantly, in the imaginations of their players. The Dungeons and Dragons game system provides a framework within which the imagination can turn lifeless numbers into characters and gives them a world to live in.

Dungeons and Dragons (D&D) is a role-playing game: players choose one of their number to be the Dungeon Master or D.M., a sort of referee, and the rest each create a character, an imaginary person or creature defined in terms of randomly generated physical and mental attributes (such as Strength, Intelligence and Charisma – see Chapter 2). The player also fills in such details as the name, sex, age, height and weight. When this is done the player will have a fairly complete description of his character, yet it is still lifeless. This is where the role-playing begins: he 'assumes' the personality of the character and directs its actions. A character, on its own, can do nothing, but with a player the character can live and adventure in a world which the D.M. has created and populated with fabulous and mythical creatures.

The game can be regarded as a conversation between the D.M. and the players, the former describing what is happening to the characters ('You are standing in a ten-foot-wide passageway; ahead is a solid oaken door with intricate stone carvings round the frame . . .'), the latter describing their actions ('All right, I'll kick the door down'). The D.M. needs to have a good imagination, the ability to think fast (it seems that you can get away with anything as long as you can justify it) and to sound plausible. The players, to quote the inventor, Gary Gygax, need 'imaginative, retentive memory, [to be] competitive, co-operative, thorough, bold, but not rash, and quick-thinking'. It is important to realize that there is no winning or losing in D&D and other role-playing games. Characters acquire gold and other treasure adventuring and are awarded 'experience points' by the D.M. both for this and for killing monsters. Ingenuity and bravery will also be rewarded. As these experience points accumulate so do the character's capabilities. Progress is measured in terms of 'experience levels', starting at first level and working upwards through second and third, perhaps ultimately as far as thirty-sixth, with a second-level character being more powerful than a first-level one and so on. Survival and self-aggrandizement constitute success in D&D.

The world of Dungeons and Dragons is a fantasy one. The technology of the game is roughly medieval, the most advanced weapon being the heavy crossbow. There is, however, the important addition of magic, bringing with it an assortment of spells, from lightning bolts to levitation, and many magical items ranging from vorpal swords to elven cloaks, from wands of fear to rings of invisibility. Another significant addition is the existence of fearsome monsters. Many of these are humanoid: besides men and women, it is common to find elves, dwarves, halflings (like Gripper), gnomes and, less loved by adventurers, goblins, hobgoblins, orcs and kobolds. Further afield are the rarer trolls, ogres and giants. Particularly loathed are the 'undead', creatures such as skeletons, ghouls, spectres and vampires: the stuff of nightmare. Not even faintly human are the more powerful creatures, the werewolves, rocs, green slime, hellhounds and, above all, the dragons.

These creatures' lairs are often hidden deep below ground, in labyrinthine complexes full of twisting corridors, secret passages and, nearly always, traps. These are the dungeons of the title. The adventurers journey into these mazes in search of gold and jewels and attempt to carry them off while surviving any dangers, whether monsters or traps, which the D.M. has placed in their way. In Basic D&D all adventures take place in dungeons, although if the group progresses to Expert or Advanced D&D, which are more complex and detailed forms of the game, they can also occur in towns, in wilderness areas (on the way to the dungeon?), at-sea, in fact anywhere in the world – or in any other world. Fritz Leiber described the fantasy genre as 'sword and sorcery' – a description which few sessions of D&D fail to live up to.

D&D as a game is the end product of a simultaneous upsurge in fantasy, prompted by books such as Tolkien's *Lord of the Rings*, and in wargaming of the traditional sort, with armies of metal models fighting on table tops according to strict rules. These table-top battles were usually of historical periods – Second World War, Napoleonic or medieval – but some gamers introduced armies of dwarves, goblins and elves, among others, into ancient period games. The Wargames Research Group added a fantasy supplement to their Ancient Wargames rulebook.

In Wisconsin, Gary Gygax and others published *Chainmail*, a book of medieval period rules with some fantasy elements. Together with Dave Arneson, Gygax began a campaign set in a dungeon called Greyhawk. The rules were published as *Dungeons and Dragons* by Gygax's company, Tactical Studies Rules (T.S.R.). The first printing in 1974 sold out in a year, and the game spread in popularity via universities, games conventions, science fiction conventions and suchlike, and was selling as rapidly as many family games by the end of the 1970s.

As far as clarity is concerned, the original rules were not all that they might have been, and so supplements, five in all, were issued to bolt on additional rules or call back ill-considered ones. Eventually, prompted perhaps by the flood of imitations with less originality but more clarity, T.S.R. issued the Basic rulebook, culled from D&D and the supplements, edited by J. E. Holmes. A year after this release in 1977 T.S.R. also issued Advanced Dungeons and Dragons as a set of three books (the *Player's Handbook*, the *Dungeon Master's Guide* and the *Monster Manual*), with extras like the *Fiend Folio* and *Deities and Demi-gods* being published later. Basic D&D was reorganized and re-released as the red-covered booklet now generally available. Further complexity is introduced in the blue Expert rulebook, which can be added to the Basic book and which provides rules for higher-experience levels (fourth to fifteenth). A further companion rulebook is planned by T.S.R., which will bring levels up to the thirty-sixth.

If you already have a copy of the Basic rulebook, *What Is Dungeons and Dragons?* will act as a useful companion to it, providing advice and extensive hints on good play, together with clarification of certain points in the rules. If you do not possess a copy of the Basic book, this book will serve as a useful introduction to role-playing and especially Dungeons and Dragons. It must, however, be stressed that this is not a rule book and does not contain all that is necessary to play. If you decide to buy Basic D&D this book will help you in learning to play it well and progressing to either Expert or Advanced D&D, should you wish to do so. D&D in any form is the culmination of developments both in fantasy and in wargaming, but the end result is something quite unique.

✠ ONE ✠

Getting started

Unlike most games, D&D cannot be played immediately on purchase. One reason for this is that the rules are long and complicated and may contain concepts which will be unfamiliar and, initially, hard to grasp. Another stems from the very nature of the game. In role-playing games there is no winning or losing as such, unless the character is killed, only constant progress in terms of experience levels, which will be discussed in Chapter 3. Hence there is no logical point at which the game may be concluded and a winner declared. The game, then, may continue as long as the participants desire. A game of this type, evidently, cannot be played at one sitting in the way that many other games can. It is played, instead, in sessions of anything from about half an hour to a whole day in length. The first session of any campaign (a continuing series of sessions in which the players take part in adventures within the same fantasy world) will probably need at least three hours to allow for character generation and for the D.M. to explain the background of his world to the character players. Before the first session, however, it is necessary to select a referee (the D.M.), who will create the world and in particular the dungeons in which most adventures will take place. He will also supervise character generation and take charge of the game in general, including playing the roles of any characters or monsters not controlled by players and administering the rules. It should be noted here that the game is not a contest between the players and the D.M. – he is not simply trying to kill them off. Unlike referees in football or umpires in cricket, the D.M. takes an active part in the game, not simply that of a neutral observer seeing that the players do not break the rules. The players take on the personality, when role-playing, of an inhabitant of the D.M.'s fantasy world. This personality can range from one exactly the same as, to one totally removed from, that of its player. So, while imagination is helpful to a player, it is not absolutely essential, whereas it is crucial for the Dungeon Master in performing his various duties during the game.

Having selected the D.M. it is important that all players should familiarize themselves with the rules so that they will have a rough idea of what to expect. The best number of players to begin with is five: four character players and the D.M. Four, six and seven players also make for good games, but three or less is not a good number to begin with since it reduces the possibilities for player interaction and co-operation and thereby the fun of the game. Larger groups of eight or more players should be dealt with by dividing the group into two and having either one or two D.M.s. At the beginning it may be easier in terms of work involved and excitement to have two D.M.s. Later on, when the players get to know the game better, larger groups will become more manageable and one D.M. will suffice.

Perhaps the easiest way to learn the game is to contact an existing group. It may be wise, initially, just to sit in on one of their sessions and observe the game as it is being played. Some D.M.s, however, might prefer you actually to play if you are going to attend at all. During the first few sessions you may feel more than a little bewildered, but after a while you will get the feel of the game and become more confident about playing it. Many groups, however, already contain about as many players as they can accommodate and in any case some prefer playing with people they know. Contact with groups can be established by advertising in game shops, newsagents or games magazines such as *White Dwarf*. There is no good reason for the beginner not to set up his own group. Just interest enough friends in trying the game and you will probably soon have a flourishing game circle.

Having found people to play the game, the next task is to arrange a place and a time. Since a game session can last indefinitely, it is a good idea to arrange beforehand that it will end by a certain time. Sessions may, of course, end before this time and should in any case be concluded at a sensible point in the play and not, for example, in the middle of combat. A comfortable, relaxed atmosphere is a great help for D&D, as it allows the players to slip more easily into their game personalities. The room needs to be large enough to allow the D.M. to sit slightly apart from the rest of the players, so that they cannot see materials such as maps, diagrams and keys to dungeons, which should not be available to them. The D.M. will also need a level surface on which to roll dice, a table being preferable as he can also keep his notes concerning the dungeon on it. Dungeon Masters' shields (see Chapter 6), which contain information on combat, monsters and the like, may be used to conceal these notes more effectively.

Apart from imagination there are two things essential for playing D&D: paper and dice. Firstly, paper is needed to record the character's attributes, height, weight, etc. As the character equips himself, armour, weapons, rations and other items necessary for prospective adventurers are all recorded. Finally, the amount of gold he owns and his number of experience points are written down on this character sheet. These will be discussed in more detail in the next chapter, where a sample is given. During the game the players should always have some rough paper on hand on which they can write down anything of importance which the D.M. might give them, such as instructions on how to reach the dungeon or a riddle which must be solved to find treasure. Additionally, the players may want to map the dungeon as they progress through it, so that they may leave it again quickly. Mapping is best done on squared or graph paper, as this allows for greater speed and ease, although a neat hand with a straight ruler can map effectively on almost any paper. Before the adventure begins, one player should be assigned to map, either by volunteering or by lot. This job is not a terribly exciting one and some groups do not bother with it at all. The D.M. will also need paper before the game, and in much larger quantities, as he has to record details and maps of the dungeons and, to a certain extent, of the larger world outside. He will find it helpful to keep his notes in a file or folder so that they can easily be found and referred to. The file has the additional advantage of serving as a screen.

One unusual feature of D&D, and indeed of most role-playing games, is the frequent use of dice. In addition to the normal six-sided dice a number of special polyhedral dice are used. These have various numbers of faces and are used to give different ranges of probabilities: dice of 4, 6, 8, 12 and 20 sides are all used. Throughout the rules of D&D a special notation is used to signify the shape and number of dice being used. A four-sided die is abbreviated to d4, a six-sided one to d6 and so on. In addition, this abbreviation can be prefixed by a number to represent the number of dice being thrown. For example 5d8 means that five eight-sided dice are thrown and the result totalled (or an eight-sided dice is thrown five times). Sometimes this notation includes a number added (or subtracted) from the die-roll. For example 5d8 + 2 would mean that five eight-sided dice are rolled as above and two is added to the result.

Most players tend to buy these special dice, either in the Basic set or separately, but it is perfectly possible to make do with ordinary six-sided dice (see table).

Dice with six or more sides are rolled in the normal manner, reading the uppermost number to give the result. It should be noted that the numbers on the dice are written in figures rather than in pips for the obvious reason that fitting, say, twelve pips on a face is not very easy. Four-sided (tetrahedral) dice are, however, somewhat different, since when they are rolled there is no face uppermost. The die will land with one face flat on the table and the three pointing upwards to form a pyramid. Around the base of these three faces there will be one number repeated: this is the result.

Polyhedral dice

d4	1–4	Tetrahedral	Numbers around bottom edge	
d6	1–6	Cubic	Number of pips on top face	
d8	1–8	Octahedral	Number on top face	
d12	1–12	Dodecahedral	Number on top face	
d20	1–20	Icosahedral	Number on top face (or no. + 10)	

To simulate polyhedral dice with only d6s:

d4: Roll a d6; if a 5 or 6 comes up, roll again.

d8: Roll a d6, rolling again on a 5 or 6 as before. Remember this result. Now roll another d6: if this is odd, keep result; if even add four to result. An example: first die 6, re-rolled as 3. Second die 6: so result is 3 + 4 = 7.

d12: Roll a d6; get result. Roll another d6: if odd keep result; if even add six to result.

d20: Roll as d12, then roll another d6: if odd result stands; if even, add 10 to result. Roll completely again on a 21, 22, 23 or 24.

Twenty-sided dice may not have numbers from 1 to 20 on them as might be expected but, instead, 0 to 9 printed twice. To get a number from one to ten simply read the uppermost number with 'o' counting as ten. To get a number from one to twenty either mark one set of 0 to 9, leaving the other set unmarked, and then count any of the marked set as the number shown plus ten, or roll d6 together with the d20 and, if the d6 shows a 4, 5 or 6, count the number as being ten more than that shown on d20. In both of these methods an unmarked 'o' is counted as ten, so that a marked 'o', or 'o' thrown with a 4, 5 or 6 on the d6, is counted as twenty. These dice are marked in this seemingly illogical manner so that numbers between 1 and 100 may be produced with each having an equal probability of occurring. Players should roll a d20 and treat this as the first digit of a two-digit number and then roll another d20 for the second digit with 'oo' counting as 100. This is referred to as percentile dice, d100 or d%. It is useful for generating probabilities for unforeseen events and occurrences. For example the play might run like this: 'Hey, Ref. I'm jumping up and trying to reach the lever on the wall. What's the chance I'll succeed?' 'Forty percent, I should think.' (Player rolls 26 on d100.) 'Great, I've done it.' Rolling the number or less represents success on d%.

Dice, paper and the rule book are all essentials for play, but there are also a number of accessories and play aids available. As well as the Dungeon Masters' screens already mentioned there are also figures on sale at most games stores which may be used to represent the characters and monsters and so add an extra feel of realism. Paper printed with a hexagonal grid, which is generally used for drawing maps of the world outside the dungeons, and dungeon floorplans, used together with figures to represent the stone and wooden floors of the dungeon, are items frequently found in Dungeons and Dragons campaigns. These and other accessories, such as ready-made dungeons, will be discussed in greater detail in Chapter 6.

Having arranged a session and gathered together the necessary materials the group can look forward to the game itself.

✠ two ✠

Character generation

The player is now ready to begin the process of character generation. The character is made up of six basic attributes in Dungeons and Dragons – Strength, Intelligence, Wisdom, Dexterity, Constitution and Charisma. These will serve as a guide to how proficient the player's character is in a number of fields of activity, both physical and mental.

The attributes (often called characteristics) are, in general, determined randomly by rolling dice. The standard method is to roll three normal (six-sided) dice and add up the scores on all three. This will give a number between 3 and 18 which will, for example, be the character's Strength. Similarly three d6 are rolled and totalled for the character's Intelligence, Wisdom, Dexterity and so on.

This method, however, tends to produce characters with many or all of their attributes at about average (10 or 11), and many players find the game is more exciting when they have characters who excel in one or more attributes. To this end there are several alternative methods of character generation. The first is to roll four six-sided dice and to discard the lowest score. For example, if the scores on the dice were 6, 5, 3, 2 then the player would discard the 2, as in this case it would be the lowest roll, and then add up the total of the rest, giving a final value of 14 for this attribute. The next method is to roll attributes for twelve separate characters and then to choose the set of attributes from any one particular character. This has the advantage that the player can elect, for example, to have a character with a high Strength if he wishes to play a 'Strong' character. It also does not tend towards the production of 'Super-Characters', that is those who have 18 in every attribute. These are not nearly as much fun to play as characters which have one or two low attributes. A character with low Intelligence can often provide great amusement, whereas a character with all attributes high, having less challenges to face, will often become simply tedious. One other method often used does fall into this unfortunate tendency to produce Super-Characters. In this method three d6 are rolled six times for each characteristic and the best scores taken.

Yet another way is to roll three d6 twelve times in all and from these to pick out the best six rolls. The player then assigns these six scores as he wishes to the characteristics, one to each. Although this does not tend so much to produce Super-Characters, it hardly ever gives characters with any low attribute values at all.

Lastly there are a number of methods for ensuring that a particular characteristic is high. These often have the additional feature that if one characteristic is high then another opposite characteristic will be lower. For example, the method being used might state that six d6 are rolled for a pair of attributes; pairs generally used include Strength–Intelligence and Wisdom–Dexterity. The player then allots a number of points between 3 and 18 to one characteristic of the pair; the remaining unallocated points, which must be better than 3 and not more than 18, give the value of the other.

Of course there are other methods which may be used by players as the game progresses. It is recommended, however, that beginners start with the standard method of rolling three d6 for each characteristic.

It is important to understand exactly what the attributes represent. Strength is basically a measure of muscle-power; a useful guide to this being that a character can lift approximately ten times his Strength in pounds straight above his head. For example a character with Strength 10 could just lift 100 pounds above his head. Strength also encompasses endurance and stamina in addition to mere physical power. A character with a high Strength will cause greater injury to an opponent while engaged in combat, because of the great force of his blows, and he will also be able to force open jammed, stuck or locked doors more easily than could average characters. He can also shift rock-falls, carry unconscious characters out of the fray and be a truly fearsome opponent in unarmed combat.

Intelligence represents the memory, learning ability and reasoning powers of the character. In modern terms a character's Intelligence is roughly one tenth of what his I.Q. might be. For example an Intelligence of 13 would correspond to an I.Q. of 130. Intelligence also helps with the learning of languages and of magic spells. It should be remembered that a character's action should be limited by his attributes and so an intelligent player playing a character with a low Intelligence should restrict himself accordingly. The Dungeon Master should penalize the player appropriately in a situation where the player can benefit from high Intelligence. For example, if a player has a character with Intelligence 4 and is consistently solving difficult problems and gaining large amounts of treasure, the D.M. might rule that the character has a very bad memory and keeps forgetting where he has hidden his gold.

Wisdom is a combination of intuition, perception, common-sense and wiliness. It is that quality which is associated with the irrational mind in a way similar to that in which Intelligence is connected with the rational. Characters with a high Wisdom will be crafty and cunning, unlikely to be deceived or outwitted, and quite possibly sense when people try to tell them lies. It is important to realize the difference between Intelligence and Wisdom: a character may be intelligent enough to know that it is foolhardy to insult another character of much higher level but may not be wise enough to restrain his temper. From what has been said it can be seen that Wisdom is the most difficult characteristic to role-play effectively. A helpful thing to remember is that a character with low Wisdom will tend to act on impulse, while a character with high Wisdom will always think before acting.

Speed, agility, balance, reflexes and co-ordination are all covered in D&D by one attribute, Dexterity. Hence it is one of the most important attributes, if not the most important. High Dexterity will mean a character can act quickly, often getting in blows in combat before his opponent, dodge those aimed at him and fire or throw projectiles with greater accuracy. A character with low Dexterity might lose his balance at vital moments, such as on a bridge over a chasm or in the middle of combat, and is likely to be clumsy and hamfisted. Dexterity can help in such activities as picking pockets, climbing walls, opening locks and de-activating traps. Remember, however, that speed and agility are restricted by other factors, especially the bulk and weight of equipment carried, in particular armour. For example a character with 18 Dexterity wearing heavy chain-mail may well not be able to move as fast as a character who has a Dexterity of 9 but is wearing no armour at all.

Constitution represents the health, fitness and stamina of a character. It affects the amount of physical damage a character can endure while still remaining alive. A character with a Constitution of 18 will also be less susceptible to disease. He will be able to last longer without rations, or carrying heavy burdens.

Charisma can be summed up in one word, charm. It includes both physical attractiveness and force of personality. A character with high Charisma will be a 'natural' leader inspiring loyalty in his followers, and others will be naturally favourably inclined to him. Such a character will find it easier to talk his way out of a difficult corner. It must, however, be borne in mind that a character with a Charisma of 18 is not necessarily stunningly beautiful or handsome. To draw a parallel from real life, Winston Churchill was evidently a man who inspired great loyalty while not being particularly physically attractive.

There are several different types of function which a character may perform in D&D. These are classified into four main divisions: warriors, known in D&D as Fighters, who are experts in feats of arms; Magic-users, whose major role is the casting of a wide range of magic spells; Thieves, who perform actions involving cunning and stealth, both in combat, for example stabbing opponents in the back, and in more general activity such as picking locks or moving without being heard or seen; and lastly the Clerics, who are dedicated to a god, not necessarily even a good one, and who gain powers from their patrons, which enable them also to cast spells, though on a more limited scale than Magic-users – Clerics' spells are typically to do with healing or defence. An analogy may well be drawn between Clerics in D&D and the fighting orders of the Middle Ages for, although holy men, Clerics are still quite effective in physical combat in a way Thieves and Magic-users are not, although not to the same extent as Fighters.

These are the standard character classes in Dungeons and Dragons. There are a number of variations or sub-classes, but these need not concern the beginning player. In addition to classes there are many different races in D&D. Only four of these can become characters in the Basic game: Humans, Elves, Dwarves and Half-lings. According to the rules these last three do not have specific classes. Dwarves, short and stocky human-like creatures, and Half-lings, very small humans with furry feet, have much the same capabilities as Fighters; Elves, tall, slender humanoids, are treated as a combination of Fighters and Magic-users. In Advanced D&D these races are more versatile: Dwarves and Halflings can be Thieves instead of Fighters, and Elves can be Fighters, Magic-users or Thieves. These features are easily adaptable to the Basic game and their use is recommended because it provides greater variety and interest.

It is recommended, therefore, that players should choose a race for their character. If this is Human, the player chooses any one of the four standard character classes. If, on the other hand, it is a Dwarf or Halfling, the player's choice is restricted to Fighter or Thief. Elves should be permitted to be any of the standard character classes, excluding Cleric, but with the special inclusion of the combination Fighter–Magic-user.

Selection of race and class is an important matter, and several considerations should influence you. The attributes you have rolled are the most important: each race, except Human, has at least one attribute which may not be lower than 9. Halflings need a score of at least 9 in both Dexterity and Constitution. Elves need this score for Intelligence, and Dwarves, similarly, may not have a low Consti-tution.

Each non-Human race has its own advantages and restrictions. Dwarves are short but sturdy humanoids, bearded, with a love for strong ale and large meals. They have infravision, the ability to see in the dark by distinguishing between hot and cold objects, and, since most Dwarves are excellent miners, they can often realize, when investigating, that an apparently level passage is in reality sloping, or that a solid-seeming wall is designed to slide away. Their size, however, precludes the use of certain larger weapons. Halflings are extremely small (about three feet tall) humanoids and for this reason can often remain unseen, concealing themselves in dark shadows or thick undergrowth. Their weapons and armour must be cut down to size, but they are excellent shots with arrows and are good at dodging – large monsters find them difficult to hit. Both they and Dwarves are especially resistant to magic and poison. Elves are slightly smaller than Humans and frail of build but are resistant to the paralysing touch of Ghouls. They can also find secret doors with facility and, like Dwarves, have infravision. To compensate for their advantages, Elves take longer to go up experience levels.

Each class has what is known as a prime requisite. This is the attribute which is central to the performance of the class function. Obviously, Strength is the prime requisite for Fighters and Dexterity for Thieves. Magic-users benefit from high Intelligence, and Clerics rely on their Wisdom. A character with a prime requisite of 16 or greater receives a bonus of an additional 10% on top of any experience points he earns. If the prime requisite were between 13 and 15, the bonus would be 5%. Conversely a character with 5 or less in his prime requisite will incur a penalty of 20% of all experience points gained; 10% is subtracted if the prime requisite is 6, 7 or 8. Since these experience points determine how swiftly a character progresses to greater powers and abilities, it can be seen that it is a good idea to choose the character class which corresponds to your character's highest attribute. Having chosen a class, it is possible to adjust a character's attributes by raising the prime requisite and lowering another. For every two points that this is lowered, the prime requisite increases by one. Dexterity, Constitution and Charisma may not be lowered. Thieves may only lower their Intelligence or Wisdom. Apart from this, a character may lower any of the other two attributes which are not his prime requisite. No attribute may ever be lowered below 9 or raised above 18. This adjustment allows a player to have, to a certain extent, the class of his choice, without suffering experience penalties. Suppose two players are about to create a character each, rolling 3d6 for the attributes. The rolls are:

Attribute	Player 1	Player 2
Strength	10	5
Intelligence	16	12
Wisdom	9	8
Dexterity	12	17
Constitution	10	13
Charisma	14	9

The first player, examining the attributes, sees that Intelligence is the character's forte and so his first thought is to be a Magic-user. This character class is only open to Humans and Elves and on reflection the player decides that his character will be Human. A second glance at its characteristics reveals that he cannot lower its Strength or Wisdom by 2 in order to increase its Intelligence since this would bring either below 9, which is not permitted. The second character's best attribute is Dexterity, although its Constitution is also fairly good; sufficiently good, in fact, to allow it to be a Halfling. The player is pleased with this result, for he had his heart set on being one. Normally Halflings need Strength as well, but if the character is to be a Thief he will not suffer so badly from a low strength. The player lowers the character's Intelligence to 10 and this allows him to raise his Dexterity to the maximum of 18.

Now the players must choose the sex of their characters. Playing a character of the opposite sex is perfectly permissible in D&D; the choice is entirely up to the player. In a game circle where members are of one sex only this works quite well, but in a mixed group the experience can often prove more than a little embarrassing. After this choice is made, a name can be chosen for the character, bearing in mind race and, to a lesser extent, class, as well, of course, as gender. Returning once more to our players, the first has chosen to have a female character and has named her Hotfa Nap. The second has chosen a male character called Gripper Longshank. Now the players can, if they wish, decide on further details: height and weight. These may be useful when adventuring, for instance when the player is being carried while unconscious or trying to squeeze down small tunnels. These physical details can be just invented by the player (or D.M.) or rolled by reference to special tables, such as the one overleaf. Our table is very simplistic and does tend to give slightly odd results at the extremes. We apologize to all female Halflings under 3 feet tall. It may be useful to decide whether the character is right-handed, left-handed or ambidextrous. Other less important but interesting details include colour of hair and eyes, age and imaginary background, invented by the player, detailing the character's life up to the start of the campaign (see the Introduction for examples). All this information is recorded on a sheet of paper known as a 'character sheet'. These will be discussed at the end of the chapter.

The fact that not every player is able to use magic or allowed to pick locks may seem unfair. The reason for this is that it takes a long

Height and Weight Calculation Tables

Height: Roll 2d6

To the dice score: add 1 for Males, subtract 1 for Females. Now find this number on the top line of the following table; the figure shown below it is the Height Modifier.

1	2	3	4	5	6	7	8	9	10	11	12	13
−18	−15	−12	−9	−6	−3	0	+3	+6	+9	+12	+15	+18

Multiply the Height Modifier by the figure shown below for the particular race:

Humans: × 1   Dwarves: × ½   Elves: × ½   Halflings: × ⅓

Add this result to the Base Height taken from the following Base Height Table

Humans	Dwarves	Elves	Halflings
68	48	50	36

The result is the height in inches.

Weight: Roll 1d6

From the columns below, select the Weight Modifier by race and sex and multiply the height found above by this weight modifier to obtain the weight in pounds.

Die roll result: 1   2–5   6

	Underweight		Average		Overweight	
	M	F	M	F	M	F
Human	× 2	× 1½	× 2½	× 2	× 3	× 2½
Dwarf	× 2½	× 2	× 3	× 2½	× 3½	× 3
Elf	× 1½	× 1	× 2	× 1½	× 2½	× 2
Halfling	× 1½	× 1	× 2	× 1½	× 2½	× 2

Example: A female elf
Height: 2d6 are rolled; result a 9. One is subtracted because the character is female, an 8. The modifier is +3, which is multiplied by ½, giving + 1½. This is added to the base height of 50 inches, giving 51½ inches as the character's height.
Weight: 1d6 is rolled; result 3, average weight, so the multiplier is 1½, giving a weight of (51½ × 1½) = 77 lb.

---

time to master the basics of each profession. Once a character has made a commitment to being a Thief, he will not have the time or, probably, even the money to learn complicated and arcane spells or to gain expertise in the field of man-to-man combat. Such training in the character's chosen class is assumed to have taken place before the start of the game. The four designated character classes cover the broad spectrum of heroes, both fictional and mythological, fairly well. The Fighter is central to the group of adventurers (often called the party). It is he who provides the power and combative skill so necessary for survival against the majority of monsters. The Magic-user is the 'special effects' person; he has a limited number of extremely powerful spells which he can use infrequently. In addition, a wide range of informational spells such as Read Magic makes him a generally useful member of the party. At low levels of experience, the Magic-user has only minor offensive capabilities, but as he progresses, the range, power and number of spells increase so that, while Fighters constantly hack-and-slay, Magic-users can, for example, hurl a lightning bolt at one particularly fearsome monster, such as a Dragon. Once all of a Magic-user's supply of spells for the day has been exhausted, he becomes almost powerless, as he is extremely weak in physical combat.

The Thief is a very useful member of the party, especially when it is in a tight corner where brute force will not prevail. For example, when the party is trapped between two large groups of monsters, the Thief may be able to slip past one of them, unseen, and get help. Beware! The Thief is a slippery customer and will, generally, think of himself before the party. For this reason the other characters will have to keep an eye on him, for he may even steal from them. The Thief is always exciting to role-play because of the sheer range of his abilities. He can avoid unwanted attention by hiding in shadows or moving silently. He can pick locks, and find and de-activate traps; he can avoid pursuers by scaling sheer surfaces and always keep himself in money by a little judicious pickpocketing. Finally, the Thief can sneak up on his opponents and stab them in the back with devastating effect.

The Cleric is back-up man for the party. He is useful in physical combat, even if not specifically trained for it. From second level onwards, he acquires spells of a slightly different sort from those of Magic-users. In general, these spells are defensive or medicinal in nature and so the party will often turn to the Cleric when injured or in need of rest. The Cleric also has the ability to Turn Undead and force them to flee – a useful defence against monsters which are either resistant to certain forms of magic or cannot be hit by normal weapons. The party might not have silvered or magical weapons, which are effective against such creatures, and, without a Cleric, the party would almost certainly lose at least one member.

It can be seen, then, that players must work as a team when selecting classes for their characters, and must bear in mind that a well-balanced party with at least one member from each class, if this is possible, stands the best chance of survival.

It is easy for the beginner to D&D to see these classes as stereotyped, but even a cursory look at a wide range of fighting men, comparing, for instance, Hercules with Sir Lancelot, shows this not to be so. This is clearly true of the other classes as well; for example, there is a marked difference between Friar Tuck and the priests of ancient times, such as Laocoön.

If you still feel overly restricted by these classes, there is nothing to prevent you designing your own. It is, however, very easy merely to produce new versions of the old classes, with extra abilities included. This is done in Advanced D&D, where the four basic character classes are expanded and include new sub-classes: for example, the Magic-user class covers, in addition, the Illusionist, an expert in the arts of magical deception and trickery. With extra powers come disadvantages and restrictions. The Illusionist, for example, must have an Intelligence of 15 or greater and a Dexterity not less than 16. His spells, also, have little real offensive potential, relying instead on fear and confusion.

Two good places to look for inspiration are in fiction and legend, for these provide guidelines and a base from which to work. Two good examples are the Houri and the Barbarian, published in Games Workshop's magazine *White Dwarf*. Interestingly, and perhaps not surprisingly, the prime requisites for these classes are respectively Charisma and Constitution, the two characteristics not required by any of the original four classes. The Houri, or Nymph of Paradise, although a sub-class of Magic-user, introduced a complete set of spells, both original and suitable for the class speciality. The Barbarian, which had some similarities with other classes, introduced the concept of catching hurled projectiles and fearlessness in combat.

Some players might like to role-play monsters such as Goblins or Green Dragons. This is all right for the experienced player, so long as it is remembered that, for example, a player-Dragon would have to start about as powerful as a first-level character. It must also be borne in mind that the average innkeeper objects to having to put up a Dragon for the night!

The next step in character generation is the choice of alignment. This is a combination of a philosophy and a way of life. In the simplified world of Basic D&D, there are three alignments: Lawful, Chaotic and, between these two, Neutral.

The Lawful character tends to view the group as more important than any of its individuals. He believes, therefore, that there must be rules. He will fight for the party, even if this means putting himself in great danger. He will also obey rules except when under extreme duress, and even then probably follows a personal code of conduct. For example, if someone kills his brother, a Lawful person might feel bound, by what he feels is right, to seek out and kill the murderer, even if this would involve sacrificing his own life. A Lawful character would also keep his promises, but this is not as disadvantageous as it seems, for, in general, he is more likely to be trusted and hence build up a circle of friends.

A Neutral person thinks solely of himself. In any situation he will act only if it is to his advantage. Remember, however, that this advantage may be long-term as well as short-term, so he will fight for the party when not in danger of being killed, in order to gain the confidence of the group or if large sums of money are at stake. He will obey laws if they do not really restrict him, but will not feel any qualms about breaking them. If somebody killed his brother, the Neutral would like to strike back for his own security and to show that he is not to be messed about. If, however, the odds are against him, he will let the matter drop.

The Chaotic character, in contrast, believes in the rights of the individual and that the world is ruled by luck rather than by people's actions. He will break laws given any opportunity and often without good reason. He will act unpredictably, carrying out his every whim, regardless of the consequences. If somebody killed the Chaotic's brother (always presuming it wasn't the Chaotic himself), then in his anger he might just wander out into the street and set upon the nearest passer-by, even if this happened to be his other brother! Obviously, Chaotics tend not to be trusted, and if they have any friends will probably not keep them for long.

It might be helpful to view alignment as a straight line running from Absolute Chaos to Total Lawfulness; the line is divided into three equal parts, Law, Neutrality and Chaos. The areas around the dividing lines are somewhat blurred, with elements of both alignments. If a player chooses to be, say, Lawful he is not necessarily at the extreme and may be anywhere along the line within the Law section. However, if his actions are, in the opinion of the D.M., too Chaotic or Neutral – if, for example, he steals money belonging to other members of the party – he will move into the grey area or even beyond into Neutrality. In this case, he will be penalized by the D.M. and will be forced to change alignment.

The Basic rules suggest that there is little difference between Lawful and 'good' behaviour and between Chaotic and 'evil' behaviour. This is evidently a gross over-simplification: it is perfectly possible for there to be Lawful evil or Chaotic good people. The Daleks in the television series *Dr Who*, for example, are obviously Lawful evil, while the Doctor himself is Chaotic good. Another person who is good and yet not Lawful is Robin Hood.

The choice of alignment is one of the most important in the game. The choice is, for the most part, up to you, but a few things might influence you. By D&D standards, our society is Lawful but with some Neutral tendencies, and it is often, therefore, easier to role-play a Lawful person than a Chaotic one. Conversely, some players find excitement in playing an alignment opposed to their own natural tendencies. Also, members of a Lawful party will obviously have more trust in each other and tend to stick together longer than a group which contains selfish Neutrals and unpredictable Chaotics.

The abilities and nature of the Thief character class are such that he will always be looking for an opportunity to make a profit or gain an advantage. This will make it natural for him to perform Neutral or perhaps Chaotic actions and so you should be very wary of playing a Lawful Thief unless there are good reasons to the contrary. One possible way in which a Lawful Thief might operate would be to hire himself to victims of other Thieves and, for a fee, retrieve the goods which had been stolen.

Returning to our players, they have been joined by a third player who has already rolled his character's attributes and named him Slammer Kyntire (Strength 18, Intelligence 10, Wisdom 10, Dexterity 9, Constitution 11 and Charisma 10. Male, Human, Fighter). It is decided that Slammer will be Lawful, while Hotfa and Gripper are both to be Neutral.

As well as applying to individuals, alignment can be used to describe villages, towns or even whole countries. This represents the type of political system which exists there and normally the alignment of the strongest group within it. This does not mean, however, that every person in a Chaotic society is of Chaotic alignment: for instance, a number of Lawful groups struggling for overall supremacy creates a Chaotic situation.

Monsters, too, have an alignment which may influence their actions. For example, a group of Lawful monsters will co-operate with each other to a great extent, and will attack in an ordered fashion. They will fight to defend their rightful territory, at whatever cost. If a party attacks the lair of Chaotic monsters, such as Goblins, the adventurers are more likely to surprise the creatures and when a response comes it will be disjointed, those arriving early on the scene not waiting for support.

Members of each alignment are able to communicate with each other by means of an alignment language, a combination of speech and hand signals. In general, only a member of the same alignment as the person communicating will understand him, but onlookers of different alignments will realize what language he is speaking. These languages are very limited, however, the vocabulary restricting topics of conversation mainly to those of a religious or philosophical nature. For day-to-day usage, other languages are spoken. All characters know the Common Tongue. This has, ostensibly, grown up throughout many centuries with the attempts of the various races to communicate with each other. In fact, it is a convenient game device to avoid awkward situations in which player-characters could not understand each other. Such situations would make it difficult, if not impossible, for characters of different races to work together and would, therefore, destroy the flow of the game. Nevertheless, the non-Human races do still have their own particular languages. In addition to their own tongue, common and alignment languages, all Elves can also speak the languages of the following monsters: Orcs, Hobgoblins and Gnolls. Similarly, Dwarves speak Gnome, Kobold and Goblin as additional languages while Halflings can only speak Common and their own racial and alignment tongues. The Intelligence of a character determines how proficiently he can speak, read and write his native languages, or just Common for Humans. With an Intelligence as low as 3 a character has difficulty speaking even Common, and cannot read or write. At an Intelligence of 4, the character can speak his native languages fluently, and an Intelligence of 6 enables him to write simple Common words. (Note that alignment language is never written down.) A character with an Intelligence of 9 or more can read and write native languages. High Intelligence brings with it the knowledge of additional languages, assumed to have been learnt prior to the beginning of the game; an extra language at Intelligence 13, a second at 16 and a final one at the maximum possible Intelligence, 18. This means that Gripper, as a Halfling with Intelligence 12, can speak the languages of Halfling, Common and Neutral, his alignment tongue. Slammer, with Intelligence 10, can speak Common and Lawful. Hotfa's Intelligence of 16 enables her to speak two more languages in addition to Common and Lawful. The player's choice for her is Dwarvish and Dragon. Speaking a monster's language opens up a useful channel for negotiation with it, although 20% of any type of Intelligent monster can speak Common anyway.

At the beginning of the game, each character receives a certain amount of money. After alignment has been chosen, roll 3d6 and multiply the result by 10. This is a number between 30 and 180, the amount of money the character has in gold pieces, or gps for short. This is meant to represent the life savings and inherited monies of the character and is all he will receive to purchase equipment. In Basic D&D, the standard unit of currency is the gold piece; smaller denominations are the copper piece (cp), the silver piece (sp) and the electrum piece (ep); the largest denomination is the platinum piece (pp). A gold piece is equivalent to 100 copper pieces, 10 silver pieces, 2 electrum pieces or one fifth of a platinum piece. All these coins have the same weight, one tenth of a pound. Weights in D&D are generally expressed in terms of gold pieces (or coins). For example, the weight of a dagger is 10 gold pieces, which is equivalent to one pound weight.

Having received the initial allotment of gold pieces, the player must equip his character with armour, weapons and miscellaneous items useful for adventuring. As regards armour and weapons there are certain restrictions on what a character may or may not carry. Magic-users may not wear armour of any sort or carry a shield, nor may they use any weapon, except a dagger. This is because their magical training is so opposed to the practice of physical combat as to make it almost an anathema. Thieves may not wear metal armour or carry a shield, since such equipment does not lend itself to silent movement or climbing walls. Clerics may wear any of the three types of armour, but may not use weapons which draw blood, as this is deemed to be contrary to their religious views. Instead, they use un-edged weapons such as the mace or the sling. Fighters are not constrained in their choice of armour or weapons – the whole range is open to them. Because of their diminutive size, Halflings and Dwarves cannot use a two-handed sword or a longbow. Indeed, Halflings must have all their armour and weapons suitably reduced in scale.

It is recommended that the first item a character purchases should be a weapon. For the Magic-user the choice is obvious, but he should buy three or four daggers, probably including a silver one. No character, other than a Cleric, should ever really be without a concealed dagger.

For a Cleric, the choice is essentially between mace and war hammer, and, as these two are identical for game purposes, the player's personal preference will prevail. If they can afford it, Clerics should wear plate armour and shield even if this restricts their movement (see below). After other equipment, such as rations and lanterns, has been bought, he should spend any money left on purchasing a sling, as it is always useful to have a projectile weapon. The Thief must have his Thieves' tools, for without them he cannot utilize many of his abilities. Leather armour and a two-handed sword are the best combination for him, since he cannot use a shield anyway. A longbow and arrows will also prove useful, if money allows. Fighters should wear plate armour, if at all possible, but their choice of weapon poses a problem. A two-handed sword, the most powerful weapon in Basic D&D, cannot be used with a shield, and so a character with such a weapon will be protected less well. Therefore, the Fighter may opt for either the defensive combination of normal sword and shield, or the more offensive two-handed sword by itself. He, too, would be well advised to carry a bow.

As well as this specialized equipment, there are a number of items of more general use. A backpack is probably the most efficient way of carrying many of the smaller of these without greatly restricting movement, and, as such, is a must for virtually every character. Some sort of sack is also necessary for carrying any gold or other treasure recovered in the dungeon. A small sack will carry 200 gold pieces in weight, while a large sack carries 600 gold pieces.

Most dungeons are badly lit, if at all, since the majority of monsters can see in the dark, like Elves and Dwarves, and so the party will need some sort of light source, either torches or lanterns. Torches are cheap, but can blow out easily and do not burn for very long. Lanterns are more expensive and are fuelled by oil. If put down, say, just before a combat, a lantern will stay alight, while a torch will be extinguished. The choice will ultimately be decided by how much money is left after buying armour and weapons. Clearly a tinderbox is needed to light both types, and flasks of oil are required for any lanterns. Even if the party has no lanterns, it will find oil a very useful substance: it can be spread on the floor to form a pool and then lit in order to scare off or hurt monsters. Oil, in flasks, can also be hurled at creatures and then lit by a flaming arrow or thrown torch. Some monsters, however, are not affected by fire, either because they use fire themselves, like Red Dragons, or because they have no body, such as Wraiths.

Rope is another item that no party should be without. It is sold in lengths of 50 feet, and 100 feet shared among members of the party should suffice in most cases, but some adventurers like to carry their own rope in case they get separated from their partners. Other popular personal equipment includes holy symbols and mirrors. The former repulse vampires while the latter are useful against certain monsters, like the Medusa, whose gaze turns whatever it sees to stone, and so a mirror can be used both to attack it and to make it turn itself to stone! Many adventurers also carry iron spikes, which jam doors open or shut, and wolfsbane, a herb which repels werewolves and other lycanthropes.

Many parties swear by the ten-foot pole, a piece of equipment which allows them to check for traps at a well-removed distance, but anyone who has actually carried such a pole in real life will realize just how cumbersome it is. A six-foot pole is more manoeuvrable. Finally, the adventurer must buy rations. Here, too, there are two sorts: iron and standard. Standard rations are for normal use, but iron rations are needed down a dungeon. All rations are sold in amounts for one person for one week, and normally one week's worth will be sufficient.

Having chosen equipment, the player must record where the items are located on the character's body. This is done both for realism and to prevent arguments with the D.M. Otherwise, a player might claim, for example, that his dagger is down his boot, and will not be found by the goblins searching him. All changes to this record of equipment are assumed to be permanent, unless otherwise stated, so if a player drops his lantern and draws his sword, he must sheath the weapon and pick up the lantern at the end of combat, or else he will be assumed to have left it behind.

Let us examine the process by which Slammer and his friends are equipped. 3d6 are rolled for gold and the total of 11 is obtained; this is multiplied by ten to give Slammer 110 gold pieces. His equipment is listed below, in the order he selects it, with the body location where applicable:

> Two-handed sword (in hands)
> Plate mail armour
> Backpack
> Iron rations for 1 week (in backpack)
> Normal dagger (down left boot)
> Rope 50 feet (worn sash fashion)
> Sack, large (in backpack)
> Flask of oil (in backpack)
> Iron spikes, 12 (in backpack)
> Hammer, small (in backpack)

This leaves him 4 gold pieces, which he keeps in a pouch on his belt. These, and other 'normal' items of clothing, are assumed to be in the character's possession at the start of the game.

Hotfa gets 100 gold pieces to start with and spends 91 of them, as follows: in her backpack she puts two flasks of oil, a dagger, one week's worth of iron rations, a steel mirror, a large sack, a tinderbox and a bunch of wolfsbane. There is one silver dagger down her right boot and a normal dagger is tucked into her belt. She carries a lantern in her left hand and a six-foot pole in her right.

Gripper buys leather armour and a short sword for his main equipment. He also purchases a short bow and a quiver, with twenty normal and two silver-tipped arrows. In a backpack he places two flasks of oil, a tinderbox, his Thieves' tools, iron rations for one week, a small sack and a mirror. Across his chest he has a coil of rope, and in his belt he keeps a dagger. In his left hand he carries a lantern, while in the other he holds his sword. This equipment costs him all but one of his original 140 gold pieces.

Having bought equipment, a player must work out the armour class and encumbrance of his character. It is obvious that it is easier to harm someone with no armour than someone in plate mail, and armour class, in D&D, represents the difficulty of hitting *and* injuring the character. A man with only clothing has an armour class of 9, and the better the armour, the lower the number his armour class is, so that plate mail is armour class 3. Additionally, a shield will make a character's armour class lower by 1. Physical protection is not the only factor involved in armour class, although it is the major one. If a character is particularly agile and adept at dodging blows, he will not be hit as often as an average or slow one. A high or low Dexterity, therefore, will affect a character's armour class, by as much as 3 either way. Gripper, with 18 Dexterity, gains a bonus of 3 on armour class 7, for leather armour, making a final result of 4. Slammer's plate mail gives him an armour class of 3 (often abbreviated to A C 3). Magic-users are allowed no armour and so Hotfa has A C 9. Monsters also have an armour class, and although this is sometimes metal or leather armour, it more often represents the toughness of hide, or how small and swift a target the monster offers.

Encumbrance will determine the speed at which a character moves, and both armour and heavy treasure will slow him down. The maximum amount of weight a character can carry is 1,600 coins worth, and this, according to the rules, means he will walk thirty feet in a turn or one yard in a minute! Even considering that the character in total darkness, mapping his way, searching and trying to be silent, this is clearly ridiculous. More realistic rates are obtained by reading 'yards' for 'feet', but even these are on the slow side. If a character is wearing metal armour or is carrying between 600 and 800 coins, he can move twice as fast at 60 units per turn. Wearing leather armour or carrying between 400 and 600 coins means the character can move at 90 units per turn. Finally an unarmoured man with less than 400 coins worth of weight can move at the fastest rate of 120 units per turn. These movement rates are, of course, only for walking, and different rates apply in combat or running. For example, a man in leather armour can move thirty feet in ten seconds during combat, and ninety feet in ten seconds when running. In most cases, a party will move at the rate of its slowest member, but it is useful to have someone swift to scout out ahead.

Slammer's equipment totals 740 coins weight, and this, coupled with the fact that he has plate mail, means he moves at 60 units per turn. Hotfa's equipment is very light, weighing only 110 coins weight, and as she is unarmoured she can move at 120 units per turn. Gripper's equipment is slightly heavier at 350 coins, which would normally allow him to move at 120 units per turn, but his leather armour restricts this to 90 units per turn.

The character is almost ready to adventure, but there is one more part of character generation left: hit points. Hit points represent the amount of physical damage someone can take before dying. A character has a certain number of hit points at the start of his first adventure and every time he is hit he loses some of these. If the total falls to zero, he dies. Lost hit points can, however, be recovered (as long as the character has not died!), and resting for one day will cause him to regain from 1 to 3 points. Potions and spells will also heal hit points.

It may strike the novice player as unrealistic that a character can fight as if uninjured with only 1 hit point left, but drops dead immediately when he receives another blow. D&D and other role-playing games, however, must achieve a balance between realism and playability, and it is not much fun to have a character who is powerless when wounded. There are a number of unsatisfactory ways of explaining, in realistic terms, why a person with a few hit points left should fight as if he had all his hit points. One is to consider that the first few hit points represent the character's luck when it comes to avoiding serious wounds and this luck runs out as hit points get fewer. Another view is that the character is skilful at avoiding serious wounds but becomes tired. Lastly, one can see the first few hit points as cuts and bruises that do not affect the character's performance, but that the last hit points represent the character's head being cut off or his being run through with a sword. All these explanations have obvious drawbacks and it is, perhaps, best to view hit points as physical damage where only the last one matters, as a necessary game device.

Magic-users and Thieves are not used to physical combat and hence cannot sustain so much damage as Clerics or Fighters. To reflect this they have on average fewer hit points at first level. Magic-users and Thieves have 1–4 (1d4) hit points, Clerics have 1–6 (1d6) and Fighters have 1–8 (1d8). A man who is fit and of a strong build will be able to sustain more damage than a normal man. Constitution will affect hit points: with 18 Constitution, a character gains 3 hit points and, conversely, with a Constitution of 3 he suffers a penalty of 3. Between these extremes various Constitutions will give different penalities or bonuses. A normal weapon, like a spear, does 1–6 damage, so that first-level characters are extremely vulnerable. To compensate slightly for this, we recommend that two dice of the appropriate sort (d4, d6 or d8) are rolled and the better result chosen for hit points. For example, Slammer, as a Fighter, gets 1d8 for hit points and so he rolls two of these dice, obtaining a 3 and a 7, and so Slammer has 7 hit points. Hotfa rolls (on d4) a 2 and a 3: she, therefore, has 3 hit points. Gripper (on d4) rolls 3 and 4, which, with a bonus of 1 for his Constitution, makes his total 5 hit points.

Note that if Halflings, Elves and Dwarves can be Thieves, etc., they roll hit dice by their character class and not their race, with the limitation that Halflings, at first level, cannot have 1–8 because of their size. So, an Elf–Fighter will have 1d8 hit points, an Elf–Thief 1d4 and so on.

Players should also realize that the loss of the character's last hit point is not the only way he may be killed. Some types of poison simply kill the character immediately and some monsters can turn their victims to stone. If a character was badly bitten by a werewolf, he might turn into one himself. Some extremely high-level Magic-user spells cause a person to disintegrate or simply die.

A player, obviously, cannot remember all the details about his character and so a character sheet is used to record this information. A number of professionally produced sheets are sold, but these are expensive and often badly set out. A home-made one is more suitable, since it contains space for whatever information you consider necessary and is very easy to make. On a sheet of lined paper, write, at the top, the name, sex, race, character-class and alignment. The height, weight and any other such details should also be noted at the top, if they are being used. These can all be completed in ink, as they are unlikely to change. Also at the top, but in pencil, the character's level, armour class and hit points should be recorded. Then, at the left side of the paper, write the character's attributes, one under another. Next to each attribute the player should write any bonuses resulting from the attribute, such as hit point bonuses or armour class adjustments. Under these the player should record any special skills his character has: Magic-users' spells, Thieves' chance of hiding in the shadows, etc. All this should be in pencil, since it will change. Towards the bottom, or on the other side of the sheet, the character's equipment should be recorded, together with its location on his body. This is normally separated into magic and non-magic items. Both categories require a large amount of space, since a character will accumulate more and more equipment during the game. Recorded with the equipment should be its weight, and this should be totalled to give the encumbrance in coins weight. Beside this should be shown the movement rate of the character. Finally, two columns, one for treasure and one for experience, should be drawn at the bottom of the page. Another good idea, for those with artistic talents, is to draw a sketch of the character on the sheet. A sample sheet, filled out for Gripper, is given on the next page.

There may be too few players in the group to form a strong enough party of adventurers and, if this is the case, there are two solutions. One is to give each player two characters, but this can be very unsatisfactory because it is difficult to role-play two characters simultaneously. A player may sacrifice one to save the other, which will not happen if the player has only one character. The other solution is for the characters to hire non-player characters (N.P.C.s) who are controlled by the referee. These will fight for wages or a share of the treasure. In Basic D&D the only N.P.C.s which can be

A sample character sheet

GRIPPER LONGSHANK MALE HALFLING THIEF NEUTRAL
Height: 32 ins. **Weight** 48 lb. **Level:** 1 **Armour Class:** 4 **Hit Points:** 5

STRENGTH	5	−2 to hit, damage, open doors.
INTELLIGENCE	10	Reads and writes own languages only.
WISDOM	8	−1 on magic-based saving throws.
DEXTERITY	18	+3 to hit with missiles, −3 on AC, +2 initiative.
CONSTITUTION	13	+1 hit point per hit die.
CHARISMA	9	Max. no. of retainers: 4. Morale of retainers: 7.

THIEVISH ABILITIES

Open locks	15%	Climb sheer surfaces	87%
Find/remove traps	10%	Hide in shadows	10%
Pick pockets	20%	Hear noise	
Move silently	20%		

EQUIPMENT

Normal   Encumbrance (in coins)

Leather armour		200
Short sword	in right hand	30
Short bow	on back	30
Quiver (20 normal, 2 silver)	on back	10
Dagger	in belt	
2 flasks of oil	in backpack	
Tinderbox	in backpack	
Iron rations (1 week)	in backpack	
Small sack	in backpack	
Mirror	in backpack	
Rope (50 ft)	across chest	
Lantern	in left hand	
Backpack	on back	

Magical

None

treasure 1
Total encumbrance 351

MOVEMENT RATE 90 units/turn

TREASURE   EXPERIENCE

pps	gps	eps	sps	cps	points needed for next level
	1				1,200
					points gained so far

hired are of the standard character-classes and races, and may not be of higher level than the character hiring them.

To hire an N.P.C. the characters must pay for an advertisement in an inn or at a village gathering place. The D.M. then creates the personalities of N.P.C.s who come to see the party. The party may then make him an offer, and the D.M. rolls to see if it is accepted. The best N.P.C.s are those which are of alignment compatible with the party and which will fill in any weaknesses; for example, if a party has no Thief, a N.P.C. Thief will be a good choice.

These characters should not be treated as third-rate citizens or mindless robots. Many players try to use them as testing machines, making them taste unknown potions or open potentially trapped chests. The D.M. should not allow this and he should play N.P.C.s by their intelligence and other attributes. N.P.C.s will not necessarily fight to the death, and their loyalty and morale depend upon the Charisma of their employer and his treatment of them.

Apart from those hired for an adventure, the party will meet a number of other N.P.C.s. Down the dungeon, there may be an N.P.C., or even a party of them, wandering about with, perhaps, the same objective as the player-characters. It is not a good idea to charge into battle straightaway with any monsters, and especially not with N.P.C.s. They are almost certain to speak Common, and since, on average, they are more intelligent than normal monsters, negotiation is probably a better course. Indeed, many N.P.C.s will prove more useful alive than dead. Above ground the party will meet N.P.C.s in the guise of innkeepers, shopkeepers, armourers and so on. All these non-player characters are played by the referee, who will take on their personalities in a similar, but more limited, way to that in which the players assume their characters' personalities.

Our characters decide to hire another member for their party. They visit two of the local inns and post two advertisements at a total cost of one silver piece. The next day, one of the innkeepers informs Slammer that two people have asked about the job and interviews are quickly arranged. The first man is a first-level Fighter called Karak and the second is a first-level Cleric, Zhod Thobi. The party decides that a Cleric will probably be of more use than a second Fighter and so approach Zhod. Instead of regular wages, they offer him an equal share in all treasure. Zhod's attributes have been rolled by the Dungeon Master as Strength 11; Intelligence 14; Wisdom 15; Dexterity 10; Constitution 7; and Charisma 10; the D.M. may decide not to reveal these attributes to the players. Zhod is a first-level Cleric with 6 hit points. The D.M. decides to make him a religious fanatic.

✣ three ✣

Dungeon design

The referee, or Dungeon Master, is the key figure in any Dungeons and Dragons game. It is he who has drawn up the fantasy world and he who enables the players to adventure within it. The apparent enormity of the task of 'playing god' to an entire world can be daunting and sometimes puts off many otherwise excellent players from taking on the task. Some D.M.s tend not to take their responsibilities seriously and, as a result, the campaign fades. The most common situation of all, however, is that of the beginning D.M., who makes frequent mistakes because of his ignorance of the rules and is unable to cope adequately with all that Dungeon Mastering entails. This need not happen if the D.M. has the benefit of good advice and manages to run his campaign in an ordered and exciting fashion from the first.

Even if you are intending to set up your own group, it is still a good idea to have seen a game in progress beforehand. If there are no local gaming groups which would allow you to attend for a session or two, there are still the large gaming conventions where it is often possible to see games being played (the two largest conventions in England are Dragonmeet and Games Day). If the opportunity presents, meeting other D.M.s in your area may be a good idea, as they can give practical advice and alert you to awkward situations which often face the beginner. Such contacts are useful later, as informal exchanges of ideas on monsters, tricks, traps and running the game can prove invaluable to any Dungeon Master.

The first thing to realize as a D.M. is that the success or failure of D&D as a game depends to a great extent on you. A D.M. who is unsure of even the basic mechanics of the game slows things down to an intolerable pace. It might also be pointed out here that players have an alarming tendency to blame almost everything on the D.M., but as long as you give them little to complain about, you will have the satisfaction of having given the group an enjoyable session, as well as having seen your very own creation in action.

The Basic Dungeons and Dragons rulebook is designed to be as quickly comprehensible as possible. Nevertheless, it is important that the beginning D.M. should sit down and read the rulebook all the way through, at least once. A better idea is to read the book once through rather quickly, and then to work through it slowly, taking time to test each of the rules as they occur. For example, the D.M. should generate a character and play through an example of combat, first without magic, using physical weapons only, and then involving spell casters in the fight. All this may take a day or two, but you should not be impatient, as it is much better that you spend a long time mastering the rules than that you should waste the time of the whole group later, when an actual adventure is being played.

When the rules are fully understood, the D.M. can progress to designing his fantasy world. This is the stage at which some novice D.M.s become despondent and give up the idea of refereeing. They wonder how they can possibly create a whole world. The completion of a whole world is indeed a massive task and one which should not, under any circumstances, be attempted by a beginning D.M. That can come later. For the time being it is only necessary that a minute portion of that world be designed. All that is usually needed for the first adventure is for the D.M. to draw up a map and make full notes on the area in which the characters will actually be adventuring. This can be anything from an ancient labyrinth, constructed to guard a treasure hoard, to the set of a giant badger. The Basic rulebook lists six common settings: castle or tower, cave or cavern, abandoned mine, crypt or tomb, ancient temple, and stronghold or town, but these are by no means the only ones which can be used. The only restrictions are that the area should be one of which a map can be drawn, that it has fairly rigidly defined boundaries and, at least for the first few areas designed, that it should not be too large. Since most places of adventure are underground, the general term applied to them is 'dungeon', and this nomenclature is generally retained even where it might seem inappropriate – the crypt of a long-dead ruler, for example.

The whole process of designing a dungeon can take quite a long time, but this can easily be reduced by a systematic approach. Materials which should be on hand are, at a minimum, paper, pencils, the rulebook and some kind of squared or graph paper for drawing a map of the dungeon. It is also a good idea to have some kind of folder or file in which to keep your notes so that they can be easily found later. There is nothing more frustrating than realizing you have lost your notes on the town which your players are about to enter.

Only when you have designed your first dungeon and run a few adventures should you consider the expansion of your fantasy world. This should, at first, be on a modest scale, perhaps detailing the village in which the characters are based, complete with inns, shops and one or two mysterious goings-on. Players can be forced to journey to dungeons, instead of starting at the door or entrance portal. Large-scale adventures into unknown hills, deserts and wildernesses, however, can be dangerous, as large numbers of monsters lurk there, and once this is pointed out players will tend to want to stick to dungeoneering, at least until they rise a few experience levels. Further details on wilderness adventures can be found in the D&D Expert rules (see Chapter 8).

The first stage in creating a dungeon is to choose the setting. Generally, a dungeon is no longer in use for its original purpose by the time that the players enter it. Most are old and have been abandoned by their former occupants. Bear in mind that the setting chosen will influence the shape and size and, to some extent, the contents of the dungeon. An abandoned torture chamber, for example, complete with racks, manacles and thumbscrews, might look out of place in an old mine or cave system; it would look much better in the cellar of a ruined tower or perhaps as an annexe to a temple of an evil god. Also, if you intend, later on, to expand the dungeon by adding new rooms and chambers, settings such as old mines would lend themselves better to this treatment, as players would find themselves able to shift away rock-falls from previously blocked passageways.

Having chosen the setting, the D.M. can begin to work out the background to the dungeon. This is a very important step, for the background will determine, to a large extent, what may be found within the dungeon. The Basic rulebook gives ten scenarios around which a dungeon may be modelled. These range from 'Exploring the Unknown' to 'Investigating a Chaotic Outpost' or 'Rescuing Prisoners'. The range given is large enough for a D.M. to produce quite a few settings without having to look elsewhere for inspiration. Once a setting and a scenario have been chosen, the D.M. can further elaborate the background of the dungeon. Suppose that the D.M. has chosen Scenario 5 in the Basic rulebook, 'Visiting a Lost Shrine'. This is elaborated as follows: 'To remove a curse or recover a sacred item, the players must travel to a shrine which has been lost for ages. The characters usually have only a rough idea of its location.' The D.M. picks as his setting Number 1: Ancient Temple. He can now work out the background to the dungeon. One of the reasons for having a scenario and setting is to keep the dungeon from becoming simply a succession of monsters to be killed, by giving the players some purpose for adventuring. In this case, the D.M. decides that the objective will be the recovery by the characters of a sword of great power from the inhabitants of the place. He names the weapon 'The Sword of the Sorcerer' and decides that it is a magical sword, once wielded by a great hero. Gradually, the D.M. builds up the background. The shrine being visited is now ruined and shunned by goodly folk. The D.M. asks himself why this is so. He decides it was once the shrine of a Chaotic god, served by priests and acolytes who raided the land around for victims for their sacrifices. He then wonders how the shrine became a ruin, and comes to the conclusion that the lawful folk of the lands around the shrine gathered an army under the King's champion and marched on the temple, razing it to the ground. Thinking about the sword, the D.M. works out that the champion owned a magical sword which had been given to him by his father, who, in turn, had received it from a mighty Sorcerer, who had forged it to fight against the forces of Chaos. The champion was killed in the raid on the temple and his sword stolen by one of the few creatures who escaped. Over the years, however, the villagers around the ruin grew complacent, forgetting the terrors that once lurked so near. The priests of Chaos were not so lax, and year by year more returned to set up a new shrine. Guarded by bands of Hobgoblins and other Chaotic creatures, they build up their strength and wait to strike.

From this the D.M. can work out the information which he will read to his players, as their background, which might, in this case, be as follows:

'Many years ago, the Shrine of Kollchap flourished. Priests of Chaos made human sacrifices and their servitors raided the lands around for new victims to satisfy the thirst of the Chaotic god. The villagers, at first, were too terrified to do anything, but at length collected a small army and appealed to the King for aid. He sent only his champion, Amaul, bearing the Sword of the Sorcerer. Together, they marched to Kollchap and drove out the priests and their allies. Amaul, however, was killed in the assault and the sword has never been seen again. Just recently, the Priests of Chaos have begun to re-occupy Kollchap and some villagers have been abducted. If the Sword of the Sorcerer were to be recovered, the shrine could once again be cleared out and, this time, finally destroyed.'

It should be noted that this does not contain the more specific details, which should be kept secret. Such information includes the exact nature of the Sword of the Sorcerer. This could include the fact that it is a +2 two-handed sword (see Chapter 4), which may only be used by Neutrals or Lawfuls, as it inflicts one point of damage, every turn, on any Chaotic holding it. Additionally, the sword emits a low humming noise when any character or creature of Chaotic alignment is within twenty feet of it. The D.M. might also decide that, unbeknownst to the players, another group of adventurers is seeking the sword. This party will be made up of N.P.C.s of roughly the same level as the player-characters, and who will, perhaps, prove the greatest challenge to their ingenuity.

The foregoing is only an example of how a bare setting and scenario can lead to a full-scale background, with details of history, people and places; the D.M. should in no way feel restricted by it. Indeed, the more imagination a D.M. can apply to his dungeons, the better and more enjoyable they will be, both for his players and himself. Extra sources of ideas which can be used in scenarios are mythologies, bestiaries and works of fiction, especially fantasy or science fiction. The D.M. could design a series of adventures based on Camelot and the Knights of the Round Table, or around the Labyrinth of Minos in Greek mythology. The characters could find themselves at the Siege of Troy or exploring lost underworld cities. The possibilities are almost boundless and although, at first, you should probably design only one dungeon with a relatively simple theme, as you become more experienced at Dungeon Mastering your dungeons can become as numerous, or as complex, as you desire.

The first step in any dungeon design, then, should be the choice of setting and scenario. The technique of gradually expanding this, with one idea leading to another until you have a full-scale background, is a very useful one and can save much time. The next stage is to draw up a map of the dungeon, populate it with monsters and stock it with treasure, traps and other items of interest. Before the map is drawn, it is a good idea to gain some general idea of the inhabitants of the dungeon and of the terrain around it. Indeed, it is sometimes more exciting if you make your players search for the dungeon entrance. In the case of the ruins of Kollchap, you could draw up a rough map of the overgrown ruins of the temple buildings and perhaps mark a few spots where Hobgoblins, larger, more dangerous relatives of Goblins, are to be found. This would ensure that a party of adventurers that marched straight into the area of the ruins without any sort of scout would swiftly be spotted, giving the Hobgoblins time to get reinforcements.

The D.M. should now work out some more specific ideas on what kinds of monsters are to be found in the dungeon. It should be noted that the term 'monster' does not apply only to creatures such as Dragons, Hellhounds or Goblins, but can also be used of any animal, person or supernatural creature which is not a player-character. In Basic D&D, the range of monsters is fairly small, only about one hundred, but within this there is a large variation. There are monsters which paralyse, poison, send to sleep or simply kill with claws or weapons; there are monsters of great size and some which are minute; some monsters have roughly human shape, others are hideously distorted forms of animals, and one is made of a clear jelly-like substance; some are intelligent while others have no mind at all. In short, there is a collection of monsters of almost every conceivable type, as might be expected in a fantasy world.

The D.M.'s choice of major monsters for the dungeon should be influenced by several factors. Obviously, if the adventure is based upon recovering treasure from a Dragon's lair, a Dragon will be among the monsters. In the case of the Shrine of Kollchap, the background dictates that many monsters of Chaotic alignment be used; these might include such creatures as Bugbears, Ghouls,

Gnolls, Orcs, Skeletons as well as Hobgoblins and Goblins. Whatever monsters a D.M. chooses at this stage, it is important to realize that they will have a great effect on the way in which the dungeon is constructed, the distribution of the monsters and the actual manner in which play occurs. For example, a dungeon in which the main inhabitants were unintelligent such as Cave Locusts or Giant Centipedes would be a very different place to explore from one occupied by intelligent creatures able to plan and not limited to instinctive reactions; similarly, there would be a great difference between a dungeon inhabited by Lawful creatures and one inhabited by Chaotic creatures. The D.M. should realize that his choice of major inhabitants should not restrict every monster in his dungeon; a large dungeon which is mainly inhabited by Kobolds (small, evil, dog-like men, with scaly, rust-brown skin and no hair) could still have areas in which there are Lawful monsters such as Dwarves. All that matters is that the D.M. should have some reason for choosing the monsters which he places in the dungeon. Some, such as Giant Rats, Locusts, Bats and Poisonous Spiders, need no other reason than the fact that the place in question is their habitat. With larger creatures some regard must be given to the ecology of the dungeon. If it is filled to the brim with sabre-tooth tigers, the players might begin to wonder, with some justification, what the tigers are eating, not to mention how they got there. One or two dungeons, later on, might have manifestly absurd monsters or configurations of monsters, but at first this is discouraging and confusing for the players. Granted this is a fantasy world, the players still need some kind of logic to hold on to. An example of what might be developed is as follows: the D.M. decides that in one particular area there are some Giant Rats which feed on small insects and vermin. Giant Rats are preyed on by Giant Ferrets, and so it is likely that in the same area some of these creatures would be found. In a nearby room, a man might have set up camp with the intention of snaring the ferrets and selling the skins. A group of bandits, hearing of this trade, could try to take it over, and so the D.M. might place some of these in the area. The Giant Ferrets and Rats might have been a source of food for some Goblins, who are now annoyed at the threat to their food supply. The list could continue, but the basic idea is that there should always be some reason, albeit perhaps a tenuous one, for a creature's presence in a particular place. This does not mean that the D.M. should go to the extreme of making everything so ecologically correct that there is no variation in monsters. This is very boring for the players, and is probably worse than a dungeon which is composed of wholly random elements.

The next stage in designing your dungeon is to draw a map of it. Squared or graph paper is generally best for this operation. Before beginning, an appropriate scale should be chosen: normally five or ten feet to a square. The map should always be drawn in pencil, as changes may have to be made later on. The map is a ground-floor plan of the rooms, showing all doors, windows, large items of furniture such as beds, tables, chests, statues if any, and any other major structural features. Each room is given a number, as are any important features not within rooms, so that a detailed description can be given in a dungeon key. If the area has been used for some set purpose, careful planning is required when drawing your map. In the case of Kollchap, certain areas would have to be included which were once storehouses, rooms for meditation, vestries, sanctuaries and, of course, areas for worship. In a tower, areas might have to be included for guard rooms, lookout posts and general living quarters. The best idea is to make a list of areas which must be included. If the dungeon is still used for its original purpose, the probability is that these rooms will also be employed as first intended, but if the dungeon has changed hands, or has been abandoned, the only clue to the earlier use of the room would be its shape or perhaps some immovable fixtures. The D.M. should then decide whether he wishes this dungeon to be the major one in his campaign, one which the players will spend a lot of time exploring, or whether he wishes to have a number of small dungeons dotted around the countryside, which the player-characters can quickly explore and exhaust of items of interest. The former, if well devised, may be preferable, but the latter allows more room for improvement as the D.M. can design better dungeons, using the experience he has gained from the first few. If a large dungeon is desired, the D.M. should include stairs, ramps and trap doors which lead down to deeper parts of the dungeon. So that the players do not have to meet the most powerful monsters while they are weak, it is presumed for convenience' sake that the more dangerous creatures live deeper down in the dungeon. A dungeon is divided into levels, the first being the easiest and the difficulty increasing with increasing depth.

A beginner may well find the various uses of the word level confusing, as it is used to describe the relative power and difficulty of spells, the advancement of a character in experience and the depth and danger of a section of a dungeon. With practice and familiarity, however, this initial confusion will disappear.

It is wise to design your dungeon so that it is constructed around corridors through which the inhabitants can reach the outside world or at least other levels. If this is not done, a situation will arise in which either monsters hardly ever leave their rooms to find food and water, or they must tramp through other rooms to acquire these necessities. If rooms are only accessible through other rooms, then, in general, either these will be empty or the inhabitants of the rooms will co-operate with each other. Remember, also, that a significant proportion of rooms in any dungeon is uninhabited.

Having drawn the map, the D.M. should now begin to 'flesh out' the dungeon by completing the key, filling the individual rooms with monsters, treasures and traps. Contrary to the suggestion in the Basic rulebook, this should not be done by a system of random determination, as this produces results which are blatantly incompatible. When placing monsters on the first level of a dungeon it is important to take into account their level of difficulty. A D.M. might conceivably put seven Dragons in the first room of the first dungeon of his campaign, but such creatures would certainly kill the entire party, with the probable result that the players would become dispirited, and, if such an event were repeated, might well give up the game altogether. Such 'killer' dungeons are not a good idea at any level of play. The opposite to this is the so-called 'Monty Hall' dungeon, in which players snatch crates of gold pieces from feeble monsters. The characters rapidly progress to almost astronomical levels, where killing a Dragon before breakfast is child's play. Players will eventually become bored with this style of play, hence a compromise between these two extremes is the best method. In a good game, the players will meet obstacles and challenges suitable to their level and will gain rewards appropriate to the risks taken.

On the first level of a dungeon, the monsters should be of low power, generally with one or two hit dice; a few more powerful monsters, such as Ghouls, whose touch causes paralysis, could be included on the first level of a dungeon if they were guarding substantial amounts of treasure, although if the dungeon did consist of more than one level the D.M. would be better advised to place such monsters on lower levels.

When placing monsters of the same type, which tend to live in a tribal or band-like organization, the D.M. should consider their organization further. One fairly large area should be set aside for the leader or chieftain and certain areas might be used as guard posts. In the case of Lawful creatures, areas should be set aside for storerooms, kitchens, barracks and so on. There is no need to place any monsters in a storeroom, and monsters in a kitchen would not be armed, at least not with normal weapons. If a dungeon is still used for its original purpose, such planning will be easier. It is important to consider the size of the room when placing monsters in it; if an area is a mere ten feet by ten, it is unrealistic to place thirty Kobolds there. The Basic rulebook does not, in most cases, give details of monster sizes, but the number of creatures able to live in a room is generally a matter of common-sense.

No D.M. can possibly hope to remember the details of the one hundred-odd monsters in the Basic rulebook and it is inconvenient to keep looking up monster details during the game. One possible solution is to write down the details of each monster on a five by three inch index card and keep these filed in alphabetical order. When the statistics of a monster are required, the D.M. simply refers to the relevant card. In addition, this makes it possible for the D.M. to look at the details of more than one monster at the same time. Another solution is to write, at the top of the description of the room in the dungeon key, all the relevant details of any monsters in the room. The very least which should be marked in the key are the attributes which vary between otherwise similar monsters, such as hit points and treasure. If these are not noted, the game may become unbearably slow while the D.M. rolls all these details. Features from both these systems may be combined to give a very effective means of keying the dungeon. Each room should be given a separate card or sheet of paper, at the top of which should be written the number to key it into the map and, where appropriate, a descriptive name such as Hobgoblin Guard Room. Underneath this should be recorded a list of the monsters found, with their details if individual monster cards are not being used, and any important information about the room as a whole, such as whether it radiates an aura of evil or magic. Thus the D.M. will know at a glance whether the players can hear anything if they listen at the door, or whether the spells Detect Magic and Detect Evil will have any positive result. If the door is trapped, this is the section where such a fact should be recorded. Beneath these details the D.M. can fill in a more precise description of the room, including furniture, lighting and general atmosphere.

When placing monsters, the D.M. should be careful to avoid creating a situation where a very small area is packed with dangerous beasts. This could mean that the players would spend most of their time fighting here, and might not reach other, possibly more interesting, areas. Remember, also, that about a quarter of rooms should be uninhabited. This is not to say that such rooms should not contain anything of interest: they may have traps, special features such as magical fountains or statues or perhaps even something as mundane as stores of food. Do remember that, even if a room is generally bare of interesting, dangerous or valuable items, your players will not know this, and should enter every room with some degree of caution. As well as this, hiding vital items of information in such rooms will reward those who search, ensuring that even the most sword-happy characters will eventually learn the lesson.

It should also be borne in mind that monsters do have functions other than mere guardians of treasure. The average monster does have to eat and drink and intelligent monsters will engage in other activities. The dungeon, in other words, is not a static place. Monsters will not spend all their time in one place and in a well-managed dungeon a particular creature will appear in one place when the characters first enter and perhaps in another when they return. One way of stimulating this is to decide on the probability that a creature will be in one place and roll to find out just before the characters enter the area. If it is not present, designate an area where the monster will actually be found. For example, the description might read: 4 Kobolds (80% else Room 3). The referee rolls d% and it comes up 84 meaning that the Kobolds are in Room 3. Instead of, or as well as, these rolls, some arbitrary changes may be necessary. For example, the D.M. might be using a 'Freeze Frame' room in which a gaoler is just locking the cells irrespective of whether the player-characters take a turn or two hours to arrive on the scene. Of course, after the first time that the party comes upon such a room, the D.M. should make alterations so that the next time the gaoler, if he is still alive, is, for example, feeding the prisoners. The extra realism is normally worth while, even if it does mean an addition to the amount of bookkeeping which the D.M. has to do.

In addition to the monsters which inhabit the rooms, characters may encounter monsters roaming around the dungeon. These monsters are known as wandering monsters. Every other turn the D.M. rolls a d6: a 1 indicates that a wanderer has come along. This may either be selected from the table of low-level monsters given in the rulebook or determined randomly. If time allows, it is a good idea for the D.M. to draw up a table of his own which includes monsters which are compatible with the background. For example, the wandering monster table for Kollchap is as follows:

Roll 1d6

1	1–6	Skeletons (20)
2	2–12	Giant Rats (U)
3	1–4	Goblins (15)
4	1–4	Orcs (10)
5	1–4	Kobolds (U)
6	1–4	Acolytes (first-level Clerics)
		+ 1 Adept (second-level Cleric) (8 + 2)

The number in brackets shows the maximum number of the particular creature which can appear during the adventure. This means that once twenty Skeletons have appeared and been destroyed, no more can appear as wandering monsters; should a 1 be rolled, roll again immediately. 'U' indicates that there is an unlimited number of that type of monster.

The wandering monster rule should always be used with discretion. If the party meets large numbers of wandering monsters at the entrance of the dungeon, it may never manage to penetrate the main part. They may expend their few spells, take wounds and be forced to flee. Conversely, extra wandering monster rolls may be made to punish an extremely noisy party. They should not be used to penalize a party taking the necessary precautions and performing sensible actions.

The D.M. must now begin to fill in further details of the rooms and corridors. When this is done, he will have a dungeon which is virtually ready to play. These details would include furnishings of rooms and the treasure contained within them. When placing treasure, the D.M. may like to use the Treasure Table provided in the Basic rulebook. He should not, however, be a hostage to the die roll, and it is perhaps better for him to choose all the treasures himself. Most experience points will come from treasure, and so the D.M. should consider how many experience points he wishes to award and place treasure accordingly. If he considers that ten successful adventures should ensure that a character goes up one level, this is about 200 experience points (XPs) per adventure, and if roughly one half of this is gained in killing monsters, then 100 gps, on average, should be gained by each character. If treasures were in thousands of gold pieces, advancement would become too rapid. Players enjoy the game more if XPs are hard-earned and won by their own efforts.

The D.M. should always assume that characters are able to get treasures. He should never place a treasure which he does not intend players to gain. Placing a suit of +5 armour on the first level of a dungeon and assuming that it will not be found, because it is well hidden, is very foolish, and pointless. Furthermore, it is unsafe to assume that characters will be weakened by the time they reach a treasure room. Clever players may have avoided fights and casualties. This is especially true in the case of magic items, and when placing these the D.M. should be careful to allow only one magic item for every ten normal treasures. The items placed in your first dungeon should be modest – for example, a +1 sword or a potion of healing – except, of course, when the dungeon objective is the recovery of a magic item. If players get too many magic items too quickly, they will gain a level of power which they do not 'deserve'. Such equilibrium between danger and reward should not be taken too far. There is no reason why a couple of Kobolds should not be left guarding 2,000 gold pieces on their own if their friends have been called away to another part of the dungeon. The Kobolds, however, would be likely to bury the treasure or conceal it if threatened. Intelligent monsters will tend to want to hang on to their treasure, if at all possible, but most would rather be alive and poor than rich and dead. By all means have only weak monsters guarding large treasures, but do not just give the treasure away. For example, the characters might meet the other twenty-eight Kobolds on their way out of the dungeon.

When filling in details, a number of things are crucial. A general idea of the shape of the room should be given and of the state and type of the floor (wood, stone, earth, metal, etc.). If there are any wall-hangings or tapestries these should be mentioned, as they may conceal secret doors or be valuable in themselves. The lighting should be recorded, as this will determine whether Thieves can hide in the shadows. Smells and sounds should be recorded, together with general details of furnishing. Empty rooms can be made interesting in this manner. A party might spend some time investigating a shelf full of pots and tins containing food, whereas, had the D.M. described the room as 'empty', they would have ignored it. The D.M. should, however, be careful not to include too many details, thus slowing down play. A description of a four-poster bed whose 'second leg is about four and a half inches square, with some scratch marks near the top . . .' would be boring. If the detail is relevant, record it and allow the players to investigate. If it is not, it is easy to ad lib. For example, if the players insist on knowing what colour the ceiling is painted, it is no great burden merely to say 'White'. Of course, if this was in any way relevant (the players might know that there was substantial treasure hidden in a room with a red ceiling), the D.M. should have recorded it. The level of detail should be enough to enable the players to imagine the area but not enough to bore them. The corridors can also be recorded in this manner, with details of lighting and any objects scattered around. Areas which have, hitherto, been wholly bare can be made to seem interesting. One thing which is worth doing is to place articles which are of little use, such as cobwebs, broken arrow heads, rubble and corroded chains, around the dungeon. Players often spend much time working out uses for such apparently useless items. Unexplained smells and noises such as moans, screams, footsteps and music also help 'spice up' a dungeon by keeping the players on edge.

While the rooms and corridors are being designed, the D.M. should think about the placement of traps. In general, a trap can be considered as anything, other than a monster, which is capable of doing damage of one sort or another to the party. The Basic rulebook divides traps into two categories: room traps and treasure traps. Room traps are those which affect the whole room, or which are activated when a character enters a room, or moves some object, or walks over some particular place within the room. Treasure traps are specifically connected with the guarding of treasure. If a character opens a lock on a chest, for example, he may be hit by a poison needle or sprayed with an unknown fluid which has the unfortunate property of attracting wandering monsters. An illusion of a monster may be cast on the treasure so that the characters do not find it.

In addition to trapped rooms there is another category of room in the Basic rulebook: one containing a 'special' object or creature. This is often a trap; for example, the room may turn or sink, or a block could shift and close off the corridor. An alarm may be set off to summon monsters, or there may be a talking statue or magic pools and fountains.

Traps are extremely useful devices for the D.M., as they vastly increase his potential for exciting play without the necessity of constant encounters with monsters. Traps can be used to confine characters in certain areas. A one-way door is a good example of this. Characters may pass through in one direction but will find it impossible to retrace their steps. Traps may, on the other hand, be designed to kill, maim or merely injure. They should, however, be used somewhat sparingly, at least at first. Consider a spear trap which is set off when a character stands on a pressure plate in the floor; the spear will almost certainly hit the character as he is standing directly in line with it. If the D.M. is kind, he may allow the character to escape unhurt, if the player rolls the character's Dexterity or less on d20 (often known as Saving versus Dexterity). If the spear does hit, the character will suffer an average of 3.5 hit points of damage, enough to kill the average first-level character, except for Fighters. Such traps should not be common at low-level play; a trap should inflict 1–4 damage at most, and the majority cause only a point or two. Poison traps, according to the rules, must be saved against or the character will die. This is a bit harsh, and poisons which cause temporary paralysis, a number of unpleasant diseases, some hit-points damage, nausea or sleep are effective substitutes. Traps should not be heavily concentrated at the dungeon entrance. This may sound unrealistic, but players will soon become discouraged if they suffer heavy casualties before having made any great progress. The same is true if almost every room they enter is trapped. To compensate for this, the D.M. should place traps in areas where players might not expect them, such as in corridors or on stairs. More useful, to the D.M., than traps which cause physical damage are those which force the characters into certain places. These include chutes, trap doors, shifting walls or one-way doors. These have the added effect of forcing an over-cautious party, which insists on staying in explored territory, to pass through unknown areas in an attempt to find their way out.

Traps should be used with care by the D.M.; they should be neither too difficult nor too frequent, as this will discourage the players. Placed at irregular intervals, and of a reasonable level of difficulty, however, they will make play more exciting by forcing players to keep alert. Without traps, a dungeon can become simply a matter of killing the monster and snatching its treasure. It should never be forgotten, however, that there must always be some way of avoiding a trap; if players walk three feet down a corridor, prodding ahead with poles and searching as they go, only to be told that they have been struck and killed by a lightning bolt triggered off by their presence within a hundred feet of a hyper-sensitive intruder-detector, they will soon become disenchanted with the game. Spear traps triggered by pressure plates could be avoided by pushing poles on to the floor instead. Of course, a cruel D.M. may devise a trap which is triggered off when something pushes on a plate five feet ahead of the spear itself, so that the pole pusher is impaled by the spear.

In the case of mechanical traps, try to draw up a diagram of the trap to satisfy yourself that it would work. If it looks as if it is impossible, abandon it or 'sprinkle' it with some judicious magic. If it works, and is not too lethal, then by all means use it in the dungeon. Remember, however, that with traps, as with monsters, the operative word is moderation. Most players do not appreciate having their characters killed in nine adventures out of ten. The D.M. should always temper his actions with the thought that he is ultimately responsible for the players' enjoyment of the game.

The sheer variety and possibilities of special rooms means that it is very difficult to say very much about them. They can include wishing-wells which actually grant wishes, talking statues and perhaps a gateway to an adventure in the prehistoric past. These areas should not be too common, with a maximum of one or two per dungeon level. Some come under the heading of unusual traps, such as elevator rooms, which move up and down levels, perhaps stranding characters on a dungeon level where they are weak in comparison with the monsters. These present little difficulty for the D.M. and can be used reasonably frequently. Others, such as the gateway to another world, require much work on the part of the D.M. The effort needed to construct another world will limit the use of such rooms. Magical statues, pools and the like are rather different and their powers should be considered very carefully. A pool which has the ability to change characters' attributes on a random basis is a good example. In a game where such objects abound, where a character may go up an experience level or die simply as a result of pulling a lever, the play tends to be dominated by luck. The characters do not earn what they get and the reckless player succeeds because, although nine of his characters have died, his tenth has been promoted many experience levels by luck in dice-rolls. Such artifacts are to be avoided and replaced by those requiring skill, such as a statue which asks a riddle and, if answered correctly, gives a reward, but if not, springs into life and attacks the party.

When the D.M. has worked out the final details of the dungeon he can begin to make a fair copy of the whole. At the beginning of each level description he should include details of general interest, such as lighting, the width of passageways, the shape and size of standard doors, wandering monster tables and details of guard patrols. As well as this, a brief description of the use and extent of the dungeon level should be given. For example, the level might be used mostly for stores, or it could be the main residential area of the dungeon. In a one-level dungeon like Kollchap, no such description is necessary.

Next should come the room descriptions, each on a separate piece of card or paper, together with places of interest in corridors, such as traps. When these room and corridor descriptions are put together with the background and the maps, the dungeon is ready for use. It can be expanded later if and when required.

There are, however, a number of refinements, which may aid the D.M. in the running of the dungeon. Maps can be drawn for the players' benefit, so that complicated rooms do not hinder the flow of the game. If the D.M. is a good artist, sketches of the more exciting rooms can be made and shown to the players at the appropriate moment. These add greatly to the realism of the game as the players can see the rooms that the characters are in. The D.M. can also draw up maps of certain areas both inside and outside the dungeon, which the characters may find; one possibility is that the characters find such a map among the bones of a dead N.P.C. or even in the possession of a live one. All these things are, of course, only peripheral; they will add to the enjoyment of play, but their absence will not detract from it.

Sometimes, a D.M. may become dissatisfied with the range of monsters given in the Basic rulebook. One answer to this is to purchase one of the commercially available books which detail further monsters for use in D&D. Another is to design your own monsters, which is satisfactory as long as the D.M. does not create a monster which is too powerful for the characters. Read through the descriptions of the monsters in the Basic rulebook and construct one of similar power, then fill in details of hit points and so on. Perhaps the easiest way is to invent a slight variation on one of the existing monsters – a new form of Giant Beetle, or a Goblin enchanted so that its touch causes paralysis, for example. Other sources of monsters could be mythology and fiction. A whole dungeon could be constructed using only creatures from Indian or Greek myth. Once the monster has been created, pit it against an average N.P.C. Fighter of what you consider the appropriate level. If the character is easily defeated, the monster should either be scaled down or held in reserve for later dungeons. The following is an example of what might be invented:

Rockman

Armour class:	5	No. appearing:	1–4
Hit dice (HD):	1d8 + 2	Save as:	Fighter: 1
Move (MV):	90 feet	Morale (ML):	12
Attacks:	2 fists	Treasure:	see below
Damage:	1–4, 1–4	Alignment:	Chaotic
	+ special		

The Rockman is an animated humanoid, made of red-coloured stone. It is created by the magicians of Khan and will attack magicians of the rival college, Dokhon, on sight. If the Rockman rolls a natural 20, the character hit must Save versus Petrifaction or be turned to stone. If a character tries to hit a Rockman with an edged weapon and rolls a natural 1, the weapon is broken and useless. Powdered, dead Rockman can be used as dust of petrifaction against creatures of one hit die or less. (A natural roll of a number is a roll in which exactly that number appears on the die before any modification is made. A roll of 18 with a + 2 sword is not a natural 20.)

Such a monster will be suitable to face first-level adventurers if there are only a few of them. In their lair they would present a greater challenge.

You can use these new monsters in new dungeons. It is, however, perfectly possible to expand an existing one. If there appear to be no openings which the players have not explored, simply add a secret door somewhere or rule that a rock-fall has revealed a long-hidden tunnel or passageway. If your dungeon is multi-level, you can add sub-levels which are about as difficult as, for example, the first level, and into which inexperienced characters can venture without fear of meeting perils too great for them. There is no limit to the number of levels and sub-levels that a dungeon can have; it can become a living, bustling place with trade between levels, information trickling slowly down to lower levels, and, sometimes, full-scale wars. Some groups of characters have been known to settle in such a dungeon!

If your dungeon is becoming somewhat stale, or there appears to be something drastically wrong with it, do not be afraid to switch to another dungeon altogether. Simply design a new dungeon, bearing in mind the lessons you have learned from the last one. It is wise to choose a totally different background for the second one, for the obvious reason that too much of the same kind of adventure may bore the players. Moving on to new dungeons also has the advantage that it enables the D.M. to progress to the D&D Expert rules, which include wilderness adventures, when the characters have to journey across the land to find a new dungeon.

If the D.M. decides to expand his campaign beyond the dungeon setting, the first step is to establish a base for the players, usually a village. Draw a fairly comprehensive map and number the important places such as shops, inns and so on. A key can then be drawn up, similar to that for a dungeon. Villages offer a new dimension for play, with the possibility of interaction with the inhabitants. This gives characters something to do in their 'off hours'.

The countryside can be mapped with terrain features such as hills, lakes, woods and rivers together with other villages, castles, dungeon entrances and monsters' lairs. Eventually, the D.M. will reach a stage where he feels confident enough to draw up a whole town. This can be done quite effectively on graph paper. A town of about 10,000 inhabitants, complete with taverns, temples, thieves, beggars, town guards and rival political factions, can be the source for many an adventure and hours of exciting play.

The horizons are almost limitless; from a town, the D.M. can progress to a whole country. Of course, he does not give details of each and every inhabitant, as this would take years. Only the most important people of the country are detailed, and one or two additional towns created. Only if it looks as if characters might pass through or stay in an area will it become necessary to map it in any great detail. As long as the referee has a map of the whole country, no matter how large the scale, he can get by. Some D.M.s use maps of little-known parts of the British Isles or Europe for their worlds. All these developments await the D.M. and his players as they become more experienced.

Before any of this can be achieved, it is important to have a good basic grounding in the rules and to start on a modest basis before building up slowly. D.M.s who try to tackle a whole world without first running a few dungeons are asking for trouble. One very good way of keeping a campaign interesting from the very start is the use of N.P.C.s. It should be remembered that, just as player-characters have personalities, so do N.P.C.s. The bar-keeper becomes a source of stories, for a price; that shifty-looking tramp is really the wreck of a once-mighty Fighter or perhaps a Thief looking for a potential victim. If you people your world with interesting and lively personalities, it will become a living one. It also gives you the opportunity for role-playing Humans, so that you do not miss out on that aspect of the game.

Designing a dungeon is perhaps the most arduous task for a D.M. and not the most enjoyable. The real reward comes when a D.M. sees players adventuring in his dungeon. Before actually running the dungeon a number of decisions may have to be taken; for example, whether or not to use floor plans and metal figures (see Chapter 6). The problems of running the adventure are dealt with in Chapter 5. Once the dungeon is completed, however, the game is almost ready to play. Simply gather together a group of players and get them to generate some characters. Explain the background to them and everything is ready to go. The actual construction of the dungeon is not the referee's only task, but it is his first, and one of the most crucial. The D.M. also has to run the game, which is a whole new experience in itself. Patience, moderation and self-discipline are all required. The D.M. must tailor future dungeons to meet the desires of his players. If they prefer problem-solving to monster-slaying, the D.M. can change his dungeon to suit. There is no denying that the job of D.M. is a tough one, but it is also rewarding.

It may be of help to novice Dungeon Masters to read the following example of a dungeon key.

The Shrine of Kollchap   Dungeon Key

BACKGROUND: (See earlier in this chapter.)

ABOVE GROUND:

2 Hobgoblins (AC 6; Hit Points 2, 6; MV 90'; Attacks 1; Damage 1–8; Save F 1; ML 8; Chaotic)
When the players arrive, they will see what appears to be the remnants of a Grecian-style temple. Pillars are broken down and the roof is badly cracked, but there are signs of rebuilding. The middle of the temple is bare and at the far end there is an irregular hole in the stone floor. The hole is slightly larger than a manhole (four feet in diameter) and is large enough for a man to pass through with ease. Lurking in the ruins are two ugly humanoid creatures with earth brown skin (Hobgoblins). They will observe the party from a distance and will not attack unless anyone tries to climb through the hole or if they themselves are attacked.

ENTRANCE:

11 Normal Bats (AC 6; Hit Points all 1; MV 120'; Attacks Confusion; Damage Nil; Save Normal Man (NM); ML 6; Neutral)
The hole leads down about forty feet and ends in a tunnel. Although the descent is not vertical, it is still fairly steep and unlit, and so characters attempting to climb down it without taking suitable precautions, such as using a rope, may well fall. Roll Dexterity or less on a d20 to avoid this. Additionally, any character hit in combat while trying to get down the hole must roll five or six on a d6 to avoid falling. A fall will cause a character to take 1–6 damage.

The tunnel is ten feet high and there are many stalactites and

Entrance to the Shrine of Kollchap

stalagmites along its length. After about thirty feet the party will disturb a nest of bats. These will fly at the party and cause confusion. If any character engages in combat, with a wandering monster, for example, while the bats are flying around his head, he will have a penalty of 2 on his 'to hit' roll. No spells can be cast in this confusion.

GENERAL: The majority of passageways in this dungeon are five feet wide except those leading on to the central Sacrifice Room (12), which are ten feet wide. They are all ten feet high, and walls, floors and ceilings are made of stone. There are no light sources in any passageways. Unless otherwise stated, doors are six feet high and three feet wide and made of oak. They open into rooms; and doors between two rooms open into the higher-numbered room. All doors must be opened in the normal manner (i.e. Base Chance of 1–2 on d6).

1. ORC GUARDROOM:

4 Orcs (AC 6; Hit Points 3, 2, 3, 8; MV 120'; Attacks 1; Damage 1–6; Save F 1; ML 8; Chaotic)

In this room are two sets of bunk beds (one in the north-east and one in the south-west) covered with filthy sheeting. In the centre is a large (five foot by ten) battered table. The room is strewn with bones,

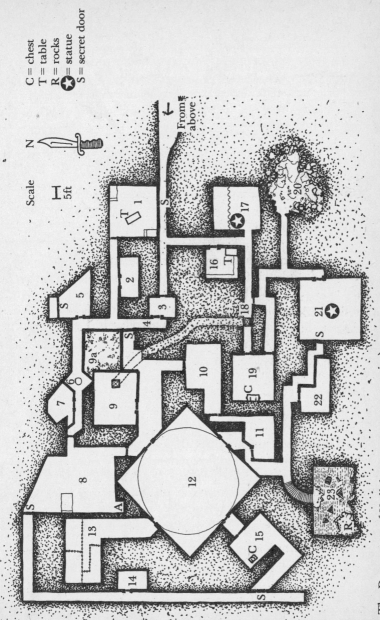

The Dungeons of Kollchap

N

Scale
⊢ 5ft

C = chest
T = table
R = rocks
⭐ = statue
S = secret door

straw and other debris. The Orcs, if they hear a party making much noise, will wait until the party passes by and attack from behind, using the secret door. One Orc will generally be guarding the door, the others lying on their bunks. The room contains no treasure other than that which the Orcs carry (2, 11, 7 and 9 eps respectively). Players will not find this unless they search the bodies.

2. RUBBISH DUMP:

5 Giant Rats (AC 7; Hit Points 4, 3, 1, 3, 2; MV 120'; Attacks 1 bite; Damage 1–3 + disease; Save F 1; ML 8; Neutral)

This room is used by the inhabitants of the dungeon to dispose of all unwanted materials, waste and so on. It is filled with broken furniture, bones, shards of pottery, rotting rope, clothes, decaying food, broken weapons and other sorts of debris. The stench is quite powerful but not overwhelming. Characters searching around in the debris will disturb the Giant Rats, who will then attack. If their morale fails they will flee into the rubble. If players carry on searching the rats will attack until death. In the rubble is a total of 216 silver pieces but it will take one turn to collect it.

3. FLOORLESS ROOM:

No monsters

This room was once the entrance to the main part of the shrine. Only the priests were allowed beyond it. The floor has now fallen in and the door is rotten. If anyone kicks the door it will collapse and they will fall through and down ten feet into the pit, taking 1d6 damage. The door on the other side is closed but there is a small ledge in front of it, wide enough for one character to stand there safely.

4. CORRIDOR TRAP:

Green Slime (AC may always be hit; Hit Points 4; MV 3'; Attacks 1; Damage corrosion; Save F 1; ML 12; Neutral)

The Slime is clinging to the west wall and will, if not noticed, fall on a party member (determined randomly). Green Slime is only hurt by fire or cold and dissolves wood or metal in 6 rounds. 1–4 rounds thereafter the victim turns into Green Slime unless the monster is burnt off (burning damage goes half to the Slime and half to the character).

5. STOREROOM:

First-level Thief (Belisarius; AC 7; Hit Points 2; MV 90'; Attacks 1; Damage 1–8; Save T 1; ML 6; Neutral)

This room was once a storeroom for the temple, but now there is only a heap of packing cases against the north wall. Some mouldy food remains at the bottom of the cases. The room elsewhere is bare, but characters removing the packing cases and then searching for secret doors may find a sliding panel. Through the secret door is Belisarius (ST 9; INT 11; WIS 12; DEX 15; CON 9; CHR 11), one of the survivors of an N.P.C. party. Starved and afraid, he is hiding here until he plucks up enough courage to escape. If offered aid he will join the party but not enter into any very dangerous combat. He will tell the party that his party, consisting of a female Halfling Fighter, a Human Fighter and himself, were set upon by a band of Clerics. They tried to flee but the Halfling was captured and he knows nothing of the Human Fighter's fate. He knows of the Orcs and the secret door in Room 1.

6. HEALING POOL:

No monsters

This pool is circular with a radius of about three feet. The water is deep (*c*. ten feet) and has a greenish tint. The water has healing qualities and, if half a pint is drunk, 1–6 hit points of damage will be healed. (Note that hit points cannot be increased above original number by this method.) The liquid, however, reacts with daylight and if exposed above ground will turn into a mild poison, doing 1–6 hit points damage.

7. COFFIN STOREROOM:

No monsters

This room is bare except for fifteen plain wooden coffins stacked in threes around the walls. Each is about six feet long and two feet wide.

8. ODRIC'S BEDROOM:

1 Ghoul (AC 6; Hit Points 10; MV 90'; Attacks 2 claws/1 bite; Damage 3 × 1–3 + paralysis; Save F 2; ML 9; Chaotic)

This room has a sumptuously furnished bed with silk sheets and hangings. Elsewhere there are various cupboards and wardrobes containing various articles of clothing, cups, pots and so on. At point A is a Ghoul, Odric's 'pet'. It serves him as it knows he can kill it. It will attack any intruders and will fight to the death. The various sheets, clothes and vestments are worth 100 gps if sold, but weigh 200 coins. The outline of the secret door can be made out but the door may not be opened unless a lever underneath the bed is pulled.

9. THE OFFICE:

Fourth-level Cleric   (Archdeaconess of Tranfax; AC 2; Hit Points 14; MV 30'; Attacks 1 mace; Damage 1–6; Save C 4; ML 10; Chaotic)

This room serves as Odric's office. In the centre is a table and chair. On the table is a mass of papers. Players searching the table will, 20% of the time, find a map of the whole dungeon. The other papers are of little interest. Just beside the table is a covered pit which leads ten feet down to a tunnel to area 18. The pit has a handle on its cover and metal rings in the wall leading down.

Sitting in the chair is the Archdeaconess (ST 11; INT 12; WIS 15; DEX 10; CON 7; CHR 10; Spells – Light, Protection from Evil, Hold Person). She has been sent by her superior to recover the Statue of Tranfax, which has been stolen by Odric (see Room 21). She will ask any party not attacking if they know where the statue is, and if so, will ask them to guide her. If not, she attacks the party, calling upon the aid of the Rockmen in Room 9a. In the north wall is a hole where the wall has collapsed and through this the characters can reach Room 9a.

9a.   COLLAPSED ROOM:

2 Rockmen (AC 5; Hit Points 5, 8; MV 90'; Attacks 2; Damage 1–4, 1–4 + Petrifaction; Save F 1; ML 12; Chaotic)

The Rockmen (see Chapter 3) are rummaging around in this room to see if the statue is buried beneath the rubble. If called upon by the Archdeaconess they will rush into attack until called off. They have been loaned by Khan to the people of Tranfax to aid in the search for the statue. There is nothing under the rubble in this room.

10.   UNDERPRIESTS' ROOM:

2 First-level Clerics
1 Second-level Cleric
(AC 2 (all); Hit Points 5, 3, 10 respectively; MV 30'; Attack 1 mace; Damage 1–6; Save C 1, C 1, C 2; ML 7; Chaotic)

This room is used by the three Clerics as a base and to sleep in. Here they perform all their meditation and rituals. They are only loosely connected with Odric (see Room 12), accepting his leadership only to reclaim the shrine for Chaos. Stacked against the wall are three bundles of sheets, clothes and other possessions of the Clerics. The senior Cleric (Kithar: ST 9; INT 9; WIS 14; DEX 11; CON 14; CHR 10; Spell – Cure Light Wounds) is standing up clasping a silver hemisphere (about one foot in diameter), the symbol of their cult. The other two (Kerzen: ST 12; INT 7; WIS 15; DEX 9; CON 9; CHR 10; and Ojar: ST 9; INT 9; WIS 14; DEX 11; CON 14; CHR 10) are kneeling in prayer. All are wearing green and white robes and will attack any intruders refusing to surrender. The walls of the room are painted with scenes of religious processions. If forced to flee, the Clerics will try to take the hemisphere with them. It is not solid silver, but is worth about 100 gps.

11.   ROOM OF ABSOLUTION:

1 Bugbear (AC 5; Hit Points 11; MV 90'; Attacks 1; Damage 2–8; Save F 3; ML 9; Chaotic)

This room is almost wholly bare except for six large (five-foot-high) urns along the south wall. These contain what appears to be normal water. It is the water with which Odric must wash his hands after any sacrifice. The Bugbear is set to guard the urns and will attack any party entering the room. The urns can be smashed with crushing weapons (maces, etc.). In the bottom of each is a pearl worth 60 gps.

Any Chaotic priest who sees a pearl will recognize it and will automatically attack the party. The Bugbear has 76 sps in a pouch.

12.   GREAT SACRIFICE CHAMBER:

3 Skeletons (AC 7; Hit Points 6, 2, 8; MV 60'; Attacks 1 scimitar; Damage 1–8; Save F 1; ML 12; Chaotic)

1 Gecko (AC 5; Hit Points 14; MV 120'; Attacks 1 bite; Damage 1–8; Save F 2; ML 7; Neutral)

Third-level Cleric (Odric; AC 3; Hit Points 9; MV 30'; Attacks 1 mace; Damage 1–6; Save C 3; ML 10; Chaotic)

First-level Fighter (Rosa Dobbit; A C 9; Hit Points 4; MV 120'; Attacks 1; Damage 1–6; Save F 1; ML 8; Lawful)

This room is vast. There is a pole in the centre which leads right up to the ceiling. Chained to this is a Gecko (a five-foot-long lizard). The floor is divided into two sections: a huge green circle and a white area at the corners. The Gecko's chain precludes it from the white area. In each of the south, east and west corners, there is a skeleton armed with a scimitar. In the north corner is Odric, dressed in black robes, with Rosa Dobbit, the Halfling Fighter. Odric is just about to drag her towards the Gecko to be eaten alive, the cult's normal mode of sacrifice. On the party's intrusion Odric will order the Skeletons to attack the party and then he will attempt to sacrifice the maiden. The Gecko will attack anyone in the circle except for Odric. If the combat looks hopeless, Odric will unchain the Gecko and attempt to flee through Room 15. If killed, Odric has the keys to the cells (Room 13) and to his treasure chests (Room 14) and also 30 gps in cash. If rescued, Rosa will join the party, in gratitude.

The scimitars which the Skeletons use are specialized weapons and if any character tries to use them he will be at a −2 penalty on all combat rolls. It requires a week's training to master the weapon.

13.   THE CELLS:

2 Zombies (AC 8; Hit Points 6, 5; MV 120'; Attacks 1; Damage 1–8; Save F 1; ML 12; Chaotic)

There are three cells, each separated by bars from the area where the Zombies stand guard. The cells are all locked. Anyone, except Odric, coming this way will be attacked by the Zombies. Two of the cells are crowded, each with four decrepit-looking male Humans. If the Zombies are killed and the party has the keys, the prisoners may be freed. Seven of the prisoners are villagers, but the eighth is a wealthy merchant who will reward the adventurers with 50 gps if he is conducted safely out of the dungeon.

14. TREASURE CHAMBER:

1 **Giant Centipede** (AC 9; Hit Points 2; MV 60'; Attacks 1 bite; Damage Poison; Save NM; ML 7; Neutral)

The door to this room is locked. Odric has the key. Inside are four copper-coloured chests about three by two by two feet against the east wall. Hidden between two of them is a Giant Centipede. Chest 1 is open and appears to be empty. There is, however, a false bottom under which there are 3,000 sps. The other three chests are locked (trying to smash the lock with a weapon will be effective but there is a 20% chance of breaking the weapon and rendering it useless). The locks on chests 3 and 4 are poison trapped. Chest 3 Save versus Poison or be paralysed for from 2 to 8 hours. Chest 4 Save versus Poison or die, in ten minutes, unless Cure Light Wounds spell is cast, in which case the victim is helpless for 1–6 weeks. In chest 2 there is a golden statuette worth 300 gps. In chest 3 there are 1,000 gps and two gems worth 150 gps each. In chest 4 there are three scrolls – one of Protection from Evil and two of Cure Light Wounds.

15. CHANGING ROOM:

No monsters

This room is used by Odric for changing into his sacrifice robes. The room is bare except for a large chest. In this there are a number of clothes, all either green or white. There is a secret door at the back of the room which leads into the rear corridor. The stairs lead up into the upper world.

16.   OLD WAITING ROOM:

No monsters

This room was once a waiting room for the oracle in Room 17. There is a table and a bench round the walls. There is some junk (paper, broken chairs and so on) on the floor. There is nothing of value here.

17.   ORACLE ROOM:

No monsters

This room used to be an oracle room where people would come with their questions and the god would answer them. There is a statue of a seven-foot-high human by the west wall. In his hands is an alms dish on which is inscribed, in Common, the word 'Offerings'. Behind the statue are red curtains from ceiling to floor.

18.   PIT TRAP:

No monsters

At this point the floor is covering a pit. Anyone stepping on to space directly over it will fall through, taking 1–6 damage. The pit used to be a tunnel but the handholds leading down have come away from the wall. The tunnel leads to Room 9.

19.   GOBLINS' ROOM:

4 Goblins (AC 6; Hit Points 4, 3, 6, 4; MV 60'; Attacks 1; Damage 1–6; Save NM; ML 7; Chaotic)

The room is very stark, with only straw for bedding, on the floor. The room smells pretty terrible and sitting on the straw are four Goblins. They will attack any party which enters the room. If their confidence fails, they will flee through whichever door the party did not come through and then return to their room by the other door a few minutes later, having run through the corridors and jumped over the Pit Trap at 18. There is a large wooden chest against the west wall which is unlocked and it contains 23 gps, 570 sps and 3,004 cps. The Goblins have, in pouches, 6 sps, 7 sps, 2 eps and 3 sps respectively.

20.   CAVE:

2 **Cave Locusts** (AC 4; Hit Points 9, 3; MV 60′; Attacks 1 bite, 1 bump or 1 spit; Damage 1–2 or 1–4 or special; Save F 2; ML 5; Neutral)

This room is a cave littered with rocks and boulders. The walls are damp and the atmosphere is humid. Amongst the rocks are two Cave Locusts, but because of their grey colour they may not be noticed at first. In the entrance of the cave there is the body of a human in plate mail. He was one of Belisarius's party (see Room 5). In his hands are a sword and a burnt-out torch. There is nothing of any value on the body, except a map, showing Rooms 1, 2 and 5. There is no treasure in the room.

21.   STATUE ROOM:

One-way door

The door in the east wall is a sliding block, with a handle on the outside but no handle on the inside. The door is spring loaded so that after sixty seconds it will slam shut and be impossible to open from the inside.

In the centre of the room is a statue of a man with his hands held out in benediction. Around the plinth on which the statue stands there are some question marks. There are no apparent exits from the room. If any character says the word 'How', the statue will speak the following words:

> 'I answer questions, three a day;
> Put not your trust in all I say;
> If your queries lengthy be
> Then I will speak confusingly.'

It will answer three 'How' questions as long as each one contains twelve or fewer words. One answer will be false (determined randomly). If the questions are too long the answers will be nonsense.

There is a secret door in the west wall.

22. MEDITATION ROOM:

No monsters

This room was originally a meditation room, where priests could come and reflect on life for hours at a time. It is now completely bare of furniture but the walls are ornately decorated with paintings of Halflings being tortured and maimed.

23. FLOODED STOREROOM:

1 Lizardman (AC 5; Hit Points 11; MV 60′; Attacks 1 sword; Damage Weapon + 1; Save F 2; ML 12; Neutral)

Sound of rushing water

The stairs leading down are wet and so anyone going down them, without taking care, will have to Save versus Dexterity or fall, taking 1–3 damage.

The first thing that strikes the characters, when they enter this room, is the dazzling light. A hole in the ceiling lets in natural sunlight and, for the first round, characters will fight at −2 on all combat die rolls. When their eyes grow accustomed to the light, the characters will see a flooded room with a few rocks sticking out of the water on the far, south, side. In the water there are broken barrels and wooden cases. Fishbones and other debris lie on the bottom few steps.

Sitting on a rock is a Lizardman. Behind the rock are 5 cps in a leather bag, and the Sword of the Sorcerer. This is a +2 sword which emits a low humming sound when it is within twenty feet of any Chaotic creature.

✠ four ✠

The adventure

The players can now embark on the adventure itself. Before giving advice and hints, it might be useful to recap on how the game is played. The players have already rolled up and equipped their characters, as detailed in Chapter 2, and the Dungeon Master has created a dungeon, and perhaps some of the outside world, in the manner explained in Chapter 3. Both these actions can be seen as preliminaries to the main part of the game and they are now connected by the characters adventuring down the dungeon.

During the adventure, the D.M. acts as an information-provider, telling the players what their characters can see, hear and otherwise perceive. For example: 'You see an ornately decorated marble pillar in the centre . . . suddenly a section of the far wall slides open and four Goblins enter the room. They rush at you, brandishing their swords . . .' The players then describe the actions of their characters as if they themselves were doing them. These actions will depend on the situation and in a passive setting, such as walking down an empty corridor, one player can describe the actions of the whole party; for example: 'We move off, with the Dwarf ahead, prodding the ground with the pole.' When one player acts as a spokesman for the party, he is said to be the caller. At other times, especially in combat, each player must describe the actions of his own character and no caller is used. The alternating description by the D.M. and players evolves into a sort of conversation.

As well as an information-giver, the D.M. also acts as the game moderator, adjudicating the results of the actions of the characters and the monsters opposing them. In simple cases, such as walking down the passage, the D.M. uses his common-sense to determine the results, but in more complicated situations, like combat, dice are used to work out the results. In the room example given above the D.M. would have to roll to see if either side was surprised, then to see who gets the first blow and finally rolls would be made, by the players for their characters and by the referee for the monsters, to see if the blows struck the intended target. There are three elements to D&D, then: the referee, who supplies information, the players, who act upon this, and, in complicated situations, luck, which decides how successful the characters' actions are.

There are three objectives in D&D: collecting treasure, gaining experience points and, most importantly, staying alive. The majority of treasure will be in the possession of monsters and so some sort of encounter will be inevitable. Many inexperienced players simply wade into every monster they see, with sword flailing, but these tactics are unwise. There will, of course, be times for fighting, but often negotiation will be the best course. Occasionally the only viable option will be for the party to leave as quickly as possible in the opposite direction. The aim of the encounter with monsters is not simply to kill them or bargain with them, but to gain treasure. Most monsters will have a small amount of money on them, but some may be guarding more substantial treasure hoards.

The basic type of treasure is, of course, coin, but there are other sorts, notably gems, jewellery and magic items. The first two are self-explanatory, but the third requires more discussion. Magic items are extremely valuable as they give a character powers which he would not normally possess. There are a number of different forms of magic items, the most common sort being magical weapons. These increase the character's chance to hit and the amount of damage he inflicts on his target. Magical armour makes a character harder to hit. Potions, magical scrolls and rings, staves and wands also come under the general heading of magic items along with a number of miscellaneous items, such as Brooms of Flying or crystal balls. It can be seen that magic items are extremely valuable and are the prize of any treasure collection.

Collecting treasure is one objective, but perhaps a more important one is gaining experience points. As characters adventure, they will obviously become more proficient at fighting, picking pockets or whatever their métier happens to be and will become better at surviving in the dangerous surroundings of the dungeon. In D&D such progression is represented by experience points and experience levels, a character receiving experience points for performing actions down the dungeon. When he has amassed a certain number, he goes up a level and receives greater powers. At higher levels a Fighter will be more likely to hit his opponent in battle; a Magic-user will have more powerful spells at his disposal; a Thief will be better at opening locks and other thievish skills; and a Cleric will gain the ability to use spells. All characters gain more hit points when they go up a level: one more die of the appropriate kind (d8 for Fighters, d6 for Clerics, d4 for Thieves and Magic-users) is rolled and the total added to the character's hit point total. This constitutes another seeming absurdity: that of increased capability to withstand physical damage with increased experience. Here again the hit point system can only be viewed as a game mechanic, necessary for the playability of D&D. Attempts to justify extra hit points are as unsatisfactory as attempts to justify hit points themselves.

This progression in experience points and levels is the only form of winning or losing in D&D and success is measured in terms of experience levels, so that the aim is to build your character up to an extremely high level. At these high levels, when characters are very powerful, they may retire from adventuring to build their own castles and may become important political figures in the fantasy world.

Experience is gained primarily for two actions: defeating monsters and obtaining treasure. One experience point is awarded, in general, for every gold piece of non-magical treasure gained. Defeating monsters, either by fighting or by less dangerous means, brings experience points in relation to the power of the monster, so a pathetic creature of only 1 hit dice would bring only 5 points, while a very powerful creature might gain the party over 400 points. Experience points can, however, be awarded for performing actions like picking pockets or healing a character and they may also be awarded to players who have shown particular ingenuity. The prime requisite of a character will also affect the number of experience points he receives. If it is above 15, 10% is added to any experience points he earns; if it is above 12, 5% is added. Conversely a prime requisite of 5 or lower will cause a 20% penalty, and below 9 a 10% penalty will be incurred. The D.M. can also award bonuses or penalties subjectively for the player's skill in role-playing his character's alignment and so on.

Bearing these objectives in mind, the players are now ready to begin the adventure. Before they start, the D.M. will probably read them some background information, which will set their mission for the particular dungeon and perhaps give hints as to what may be found underground.

Certain jobs must be allocated before the characters set off down the dungeon. A caller must be appointed to speak for the party as a whole and to lead the group. This should normally be the player whose character has the highest Charisma, but often the most talkative player takes over in mid-adventure! Someone must map for the party and, as this can be fairly boring at times, it is best to select the mapper by lot, unless of course there is a volunteer. The player will need graph or squared paper, a ruler, a pencil and a rubber. It is important to choose a scale before starting: five or ten feet to a square is generally sensible. The map should show a plan of the structure of the dungeon as far as it is explored. When the D.M. describes a room or passage, the mapper should be careful to record the dimensions and draw an accurate map. The mapper may, if he wishes, note what was met in each room or how much treasure there was, but it is important not to clutter up the map to such an extent that the general shape of the dungeon cannot be seen at a glance.

The players must now organize the party into a marching order. This shows where each character will be within the party during most movement and so it is important to consider where each character's abilities can be utilized to the fullest extent. Most monsters will be met by the front members of the party and so it is wise to have a Fighter near the front. Some monsters, however, will approach from the rear and a strong defensive party member, such as a Cleric or perhaps a second Fighter, should guard the tail end. Thieves and Magic-users do not have a very good armour class or many hit points and so they must be protected by stationing them in the middle. In a large party the caller's character should not be so far from the front that he cannot see what the D.M. is describing. Most dungeon passages are only wide enough to let two characters stand side by side and a marching-order should never be set out with more than two abreast. Often single file will allow the characters more space to manoeuvre. Our players elect Hotfa's player as the caller and Gripper's player is the mapper. Their marching order, in single file is:

> Zhod   (Rear)
> Hotfa
> Gripper
> Slammer   (Front)

This marching order is recorded on paper or can be represented by metal figures, which are discussed in Chapter 6. The marching order can, of course, be altered down the dungeon, but there should generally be only one order on paper at any one time so that the D.M. can tell where the characters are, if the players do not specify exactly.

A torch or lantern will cast light thirty feet in all directions and so one light source, at the front of the party, will be sufficient most of the time. A separate torch may be needed if someone decides to scout ahead or stay and guard something. If a scout is employed, he will probably be one of the faster members of the party and will move at his top speed. Otherwise, the party must move at the rate of the slowest member. Every sixth turn, ten minutes in every hour, the party must rest. If they do not do so they will fight badly, with a penalty of −1 on all combat rolls.

A turn of ten minutes is the basic unit of time in D&D. This represents what a character could do in ten minutes rather than how long the game actually takes. Sometimes in an hour of real time a day or more of adventure time will pass, and sometimes, especially in combat, it will take longer in real time than in adventure time. During combat the turn is sub-divided into melee rounds of ten seconds to allow a more detailed view of the action.

The party will normally start the adventure under the leadership of the caller and will continue in this manner when decisions for the party as a whole are required. This does not mean that all but one of the party take no part in the game for long periods, because the other players should be making suggestions or explaining their characters' actions either to the caller or directly to the D.M. Often the players do not need a caller and can each describe what the character is doing to the D.M., but sometimes it is useful to have one spokesman. The caller cannot tell any player what to do and may only say such things as 'The Thief checks for traps', if the Thief's player agrees. Any player may disagree with the party leader at any time and may, if he so wishes, let his character go off on his own, although this is not to be advised, as a sole adventurer would almost certainly perish in the dungeon.

The characters will normally start the adventure in the dungeon in some sort of passageway, but even here the characters should be wary. There may be monsters roaming about or special traps designed to punish those who are off their guard. Pushing ahead with a pole is often a good way of avoiding traps, but a crafty D.M. may have designed a trap especially for catching such pole-pushers. Characters should not, however, delay or make too much noise in passages as this will increase the number of monsters they will meet there.

Before long, the party will, almost certainly, come upon a door. The characters will not know what is behind the door: it might be another passageway or possibly a room. It is, therefore, a good idea to listen at the door to see if anything can be heard. Humans have a 1 in 6 chance of hearing a noise, if there is one, demi-humans (Elves, Dwarves and Halflings) have a 2 in 6 chance. Thieves have special chances, depending on their level: at first level, 2 in 6. The d6 should be rolled in secret by the D.M. so that players will not know whether the reply 'You do not hear anything' is because there is nothing to hear or because the die roll result meant a failure to hear a noise.

The characters may then decide to open the door. Most doors are jammed shut and require a certain amount of force to open them. A base chance of 2 in 6 is modified by Strength. With Strength under 9 a die roll of 1 on 1d6 is required; with Strength 13–15 a die roll of 1, 2 or 3; with Strength 16–17 a die roll of 1 to 4; and with Strength 18, like Slammer, all but a die roll of 6 will suffice for opening the door. Doors swing shut unless spiked open and monsters are assumed to be strong enough or familiar enough with the dungeon to open the doors, unless, of course, a party spikes them shut.

Some doors are concealed or so designed that they do not appear to be doors and these are called secret doors. A player may find one of these only if he is searching, unless he already knows where it is located. During a search a normal character has a 1 in 6 chance of finding such a door but an Elf has a 2 in 6 chance.

Whenever a party meets a monster, either in a passageway or on the other side of that door, an encounter will take place and the time scale will change into rounds. The first roll to be made is that for surprise, and this roll will be made only once per encounter. When two sides meet, one or other or even both, may be surprised. Each side rolls a d6 and a 1 or 2 result indicates that the side has been surprised. There will, obviously, be cases when one side cannot be surprised and so need not make the roll. If the party had heard the monsters or the characters had failed to open the door first time, surprise would be restricted accordingly. If both sides are surprised, there is no effect, just as if neither has been, but if one side is surprised, the other gains a free round of action during which the surprised group cannot do anything. If the monsters achieve surprise, the D.M. will determine their reaction, possibly using a die roll on the Monster Reaction Table. If the characters surprise the monsters, the choice of action is entirely up to the players: they can flee, negotiate or attack, or perhaps employ some other option applicable in the particular circumstances. The party which always attacks will not last long, but, on the other hand, valuable seconds of surprise are often frittered away with useless talk. The choice will depend upon the circumstances to a great extent, but generally it is not a good idea to attack N.P.C.s straightaway, as they may provide valuable information and help, if alive.

If the party decides to flee, the monsters may pursue, in which case, if the monsters are faster than the party, certain precautions are advisable. Throwing food or money on the ground may slow monsters as they stop to collect it and fire may hamper or even prevent further pursuit. If the party decides to negotiate, it must first communicate its message to the monsters, which may be a difficult task if the characters do not speak the monsters' language. Having surmounted that problem a roll is made on the Monster Reaction Table to see how the monsters react. The Charisma of the party negotiator will affect this reaction, which may be anything from immediate attack to confusion to enthusiastic friendship. The D.M. will take on the role of the monsters in any negotiation. The third option, that of combat, will be discussed shortly.

After the surprise round, which may end very quickly if there is equal surprise on both sides, a roll is made for initiative. This will decide which side reacts fastest and gets to move, and possibly attack, first. Each side rolls a d6 and the side which rolls the higher number gains the initiative. If the two rolls are equal, there is simultaneous combat, which will be explained later. The side with initiative has the same choice as a side with surprise, previously mentioned, except that it knows that the other side will react as well during this round. If the party decides to talk or to flee, the same comments as above apply. If they decide to fight, it is slightly more complicated.

The first step is to check morale; then the combatants can move. After movement, any missile fire, from bows, slings and so on, is resolved. Next the results of any magic spells cast are applied and finally hand-to-hand, or melee, combat is resolved. These steps are then repeated for the side which lost the initiative and one melee round has been completed. The second round begins with a new roll for initiative and the process is repeated. More rounds follow the second until one side has surrendered, fled or been killed. Each step in a round is not particularly easy to understand and so a more detailed examination of a round is given now.

Morale is checked to see if one side loses its confidence and flees, or possibly surrenders. It is never checked for player-characters because their decisions are all made by the players, but it is imposed on monsters and non-player characters in the party. Checks are made after the side's first death and when half the monsters have been killed. Each type of monster has a rating from 2 to 12 and when a check is made 2d6 are rolled. A result higher than the morale rating means that the monster will cease fighting, either retreating or surrendering. If a monster successfully checks its morale twice, it will fight to the death. N.P.C.s' morale ratings depend on the Charisma of their employer, ranging from 10 at Charisma 18 to 4 at Charisma 3.

The next step in combat is movement. During this phase characters and monsters move within their encumbrance restrictions. A character who can normally move at ninety feet per turn can move at thirty feet per round in combat and the other rates are similarly adapted. Movement may be very important at the start of an encounter when the two sides are well apart and the party wishes to fire arrows or other projectile weapons. Later on, when the fighting is hand-to-hand, movement may be less important. If the party does have a number of archers it is not wise to rush upon monsters; it is better to stay still and loose off a couple of rounds of arrows. Conversely, if the party comes upon a few Orc crossbowmen, for example, the characters should charge at them and join in close combat, where the Orcs' weapons are useless.

In D&D combat, attacks, both missile and melee, do not automatically hit but are resolved by a die roll. The probability of success depends mainly upon the attacker's experience level and the defender's armour class, but other factors, including Dexterity and Strength, may modify the die roll. For the first three experience levels, the defender's armour class is subtracted from 19 and that is the number which the attacker must roll or better on d20 to achieve a hit. If he is successful, a further roll is made to determine how many hit points the defender loses in damage. For example, a character is trying to hit a monster with armour class 5; 19 minus 5 equals 14, so the player must roll a 14 or higher on d20 to hit. He rolls a 17, which is a hit, and then rolls another die to determine damage; the result is a 3, so the defender loses three hit points.

The first step in missile fire is to choose a target and work out the range. The distance from attacker to target affects the effectiveness of the shot and different weapons have different ranges. For example, a longbow has a short range of 70 feet, a medium range of 140 feet and a long range of 210 feet. At short range a player can add 1 to his die roll, so that he has an extra 5% chance of hitting. There is no modification for medium range, but at long range the player must subtract 1 from his die roll. The Dexterity of the archer will also modify the combat roll. A Dexterity of 13–15 means +1 on die roll, one of 16–17 means +2 and Dexterity of 18 means +3. Conversely, there is a −3 penalty for Dexterity 3, a −2 penalty for Dexterity 4–5 and a −1 penalty for Dexterity 6–8. All these modifiers may seem complicated, but it should be remembered that at average Dexterity (9–12) there are no modifiers and, as Dexterity can never change, players will soon add their modifiers automatically. If the missile hits, the damage must be rolled. This depends on the type of weapon used and so the particular die rolled will vary. An arrow will cause 1–6 (1d6) hit points of damage; a crossbow quarrel or bolt 1–6 (1d6); a spear or hand axe 1–6 (1d6); and a sling stone or dagger 1–4 (1d4).

The next stage in combat is the casting of magic spells. Magic-users at all experience levels and Clerics at second or higher level have the ability to cast spells. Spells are memorized before an adventure and are remembered until the spell has been cast, at which time the character forgets it. Once a day spells can be re-memorized if the caster spends an hour of game time undisturbed. To cast a spell, characters must be able to speak and move their hands, so a bound Magic-user cannot cast his spells. Each spell has a range and duration which dictate the area and length of effect respectively.

Spells do not have to hit their target in the normal combat manner, but automatically hit. The target creature does, however, have a chance of avoiding some or all of the effects of a spell. A roll, known as a saving throw, is made to see if the character is affected by the spell. The probability of escaping the effects depends on the character's level and class. Saving throws are also made when the character has a chance of escaping some other unpleasant occurrence, such as being poisoned or turned to stone. The probability varies, normally somewhere between one quarter and one half of escaping the effect. The probability is recorded on a chart under various headings. When a character has been poisoned he Saves versus Poison on the chart; when breathed on by a Dragon he must Save versus Dragon Breath. The D.M. may also require a character to save versus some particular attribute. If a character was trying to run down some slippery stairs, he might have to Save versus Dexterity, that is, roll his Dexterity or less on d20, or else he would fall.

The last and most important stage in combat is the melee. The players must choose whom their characters are attacking and then calculate the chance as detailed before. In hand-to-hand combat, strength may modify the die rolls. Strength 18 gives a +3 bonus, both to hit and when calculating damage done. Strength 16–17 gives a similar +2 bonus and Strength 13–15 adds 1 to the die rolls. At the other end of the scale, Strength 3 incurs a –3 penalty, Strength 4–5 a –2 penalty and Strength 6–8 a penalty of –1. The damage done depends on the weapon used. Daggers, torches and clubs do the least damage (1–4). Hand axes, maces, spears, war hammers and short swords do 1–6 and battle axes and normal swords do 1–8 damage. The most dangerous weapons are pole arms and two-handed swords, causing 1–10 hit points of damage. Two-handed weapons have the disadvantage that the character cannot carry a shield and always loses the initiative. This means that if the party wins the initiative, a character with a double-handed weapon must perform his attack after the other side, but his colleagues can still strike first.

The results of the actions of the side with the initiative are carried out before the other side acts. So, if a character delivers a monster enough damage to kill it, the monster drops dead before it can attack in that round. Initiative is clearly important because the side with it may reduce the numbers on the other side before it counter-attacks. If the same number is rolled by both sides for initiative, there is simultaneous combat. Neither side goes first. One side says what it is doing and works out the results. These results are not yet put into effect. Then the results of the other side's actions are worked out and both results effected simultaneously. For example, a Fighter with 5 hit points attacks an Orc with 3 hit points. On the initiative die rolls, the player and the D.M. (for the Orc) both roll 3, meaning simultaneous combat. The character attacks and a 14 is rolled; as this is enough for a hit, another die is rolled for damage. The character is using a normal sword, so a d8 is rolled: result, a 5. This amount of damage is enough to kill the Orc, but since it is simultaneous combat the damage is not taken yet. The D.M. then works out the Orc's attack. A 19 is rolled, so the Orc has hit with his mace. A d6 is rolled for damage. Either a 5 or 6 would kill the character as well, but luckily for the character only a 2 is rolled. Now the results of combat are put into effect. The character takes 2 hit points of damage, reducing him to 3 hit points, and the Orc is killed.

In summary, characters explore the dungeon: at first they know only the vague background but slowly, as the adventure proceeds, they build up a map of the dungeon. They progress normally in ten-minute (adventure time) turns until they meet a monster. In the ensuing encounter they aim to defeat the monster and secure its treasure. These are the game mechanics and a knowledge of them will enable someone to play the game, but some advice is necessary for good and successful play.

The Fighter's role is fairly obvious: he must attack monsters when the situation calls for combat. Any magical weapons ought to be offered to him first so that he can build himself up into an effective monster-slayer. He should not, however, urge the party into combat at all times. Although this would mean his getting more experience points because he had killed more monsters, it would also increase the likelihood of being killed himself.

At first level, the Cleric is essentially a second-rate fighter. He has the potential for an excellent armour class and has a reasonable amount of hit points. This makes him a good defensive character.

At second level, the Cleric can use spells. These are, also, of a defensive nature but include the extremely useful Cure Light Wounds spell. This enables a character to recover 2–7 hit points. This spell can save a character, but timing is crucial. A character cannot gain more hit points than he had before taking any damage, and so if the spell is cast on someone who has only taken a couple of points of damage, it will largely be wasted. Although it may seem unfair, the spell should generally be reserved for Fighters at low levels. They do take the brunt of attacks and so will need healing more often. Protection from Evil is another useful first-level Clerical spell.

The Magic-user has spell capability from the beginning but is very weak in combat. The choice of spell is crucial and two spells stand out from the rest: Charm Person and Sleep. The latter puts to sleep large numbers of low-level creatures while the former makes one low-level creature believe that the caster is its best friend. The Sleep spell can be very effective when the party encounters a large band of monsters, since it swiftly incapacitates the majority of them. Charm Person is good because it forcibly enlists a monster into the party, increasing the fighting force, but unfortunately it does not have a 100% chance of success as the monster is allowed a saving throw.

The decision when to use spells is even more important. At first level the Magic-user has only one spell, and once this has been expended he is virtually powerless. He must avoid combat because he has a poor armour class and very few hit points, which means that one blow may easily kill him. A first-level Magic-user should use his spell only when combat looks hopeless. This includes a situation where a character is on the point of being killed and the situation where the party has met a vastly superior group of monsters. In this latter case, flight might be more advisable. At higher levels, when the Magic-user has more spells, some of which are very powerful, he will be the most valuable member of the party, but at the start he is very weak.

The Thief has the greatest range of skills of any of the low-level characters. Many of these will help the party as a whole, but some will help only the Thief and may even be detrimental to other members of the party.

For the party, the Thief can act as a useful scout. His Open Locks ability will enable the party to get into rooms and chests, and his ability to Find and Remove Traps is obviously very useful. Three abilities contribute to his role as scout: Move Silently, Hide in Shadows and Hear Noise. When employing the first two the Thief will always think he has been successful, but the D.M. will know for certain. Climbing Sheer Surfaces will often help the whole party, since the Thief can climb up with a rope and throw the end back down to the party.

One ability, Pick Pockets, is not very useful against monsters down the dungeon, but may be applied against members of the Thief's own party. With a good D.M. it will be perfectly possible to do this and it livens up the game, but often the necessity for the Thief's player to pass the requisite note to the D.M. will warn the other players that something is afoot.

When all the abilities of the different characters are combined, the party should be able to cope with nearly every situation that arises. If the players act sensibly and are not too impatient, their characters will soon gain higher levels of experience, where they are more powerful and will even be able to face such powerful monsters as fully grown dragons.

So much for hypothetical advice. In the following example we can see how all this works in practice. On the left-hand pages is a 'story' description of what happens when Slammer, Hotfa and Gripper from Chapter 2 venture down the mini-module designed in Chapter 3. On the right-hand side are notes on how the events opposite work in D&D terms, and comments on the characters' play. The best idea is to read through the story first and then go back through it slowly, referring to the notes and the dungeon design in Chapter 3, making sure you understand everything.

The example does not explain how the format of play works, which should be clear by now; most rulebooks have an 'abacab', set out in printed form in the manner of a play script, showing speaker and dialogue.

We join the party as they have killed the Locust in Room 20. Zhod was guarding the intersection in case the Orcs in Room 1 were following the party. None of the characters is wounded, as yet, although Gripper has another problem . . .

Zhod came running up the passage.

'What happened?' he gasped.

Hotfa and Slammer finished kicking the cave about. Gripper lay to one side, nursing his wounds.

'There's nothing here,' said Hotfa, and Slammer nodded.

'What was it you wanted, godbod?' she continued.

Zhod repeated his question.

'Weird,' Slammer told him. 'We came in here, decided it was a bit of a dump. We were going to go back and get you when Gripper trod on a cave locust, hidden in the rubbish. It spat on him, but I cooled in and creamed it with one stroke. There was another in here, but it hit dirt before we got it. Er . . . don't go near Gripper, doc: you'll be sick. He's got locust spew on him, and smells worse than Hotfa's perfume.'

'Say that again, farmboy,' called Hotfa from the other side of the cave.

Gripper interrupted from where he was lying.

'Hey, you know this body I'm sitting on?'

There was a short pause.

'Yeah, halfman; so what?' asked Hotfa, coming nearer to look.

'There's a map in its pocket.'

Slammer held Zhod back from going to look.

'Throw it to us, Gripper,' he yelled.

Gripper stood up.

'Don't come near me, Gripling,' shrieked Hotfa.

'I'm not,' said the Thief, in an injured tone, and threw the map to Slammer. The warrior waved it in the air and unfolded it.

'It's a map of this place,' he told Hotfa.

'Let me look,' she said, and then, 'How can you tell? Oh, I get it. What did the corpse die of, Gripper?'

'I don't know,' said the apprentice. 'Most of it's missing.'

The party left the cave and retraced their steps to the intersection. Gripper walked in front, occasionally prodded by Hotfa with a pole.

'Where do we go now?' whined Gripper.

'Left, you reckon?' said Slammer, and the other two nodded.

Gripper tried to open the slab-like door and failed. Hotfa nodded to Slammer, who took a deep breath, pushed past the thief and tugged the door open. When Gripper was safely in the room, the

Hotfa and Slammer are searching the room.
In fact, he has suffered no damage as such.

Both the party and the locusts were surprised.

The locust failed a morale check.
Gripper's clothes have been spat on by the locust, so that anyone going near him must Save versus Poison or be violently ill.

Gripper has been searching the body.

Still being careful not to go near Gripper.

Trying to remove any lingering trace of locust on the map.

A wandering monster die roll comes up 5: no monster appears.

The party seems to have abandoned the idea of having a caller.
Gripper tries to open the door but rolls a 3.
Slammer makes a Saving roll versus Poison. The D.M. allows +3 because of the precautions. A roll of 13 means that Slammer isn't ill.

Cleric and the Magic-user followed Slammer through the doorway.

'Is it safe?' asked Zhod.

'Yeah, I reckon so,' Hotfa reassured him. 'We should have checked though.'

There was a large stone statue in the centre of the room, of a man, standing, his hands held out in benediction. He stood on a plinth, which had barely distinguishable question marks on it.

'Maybe if I prise the head off . . .,' suggested Gripper.

'Shut up, vandal,' said Hotfa, and then as an afterthought, 'and stand in the corner and wilt.'

Gripper maintained an injured silence on the far side of the room while the other three inspected the statue. At a rumbling sound, they looked round to see the door slide shut with a thud. Slammer leapt to the doorway and tried to force it open.

'It's hopeless,' he reported. 'There's no handle this side.'

Zhod heaved at the door.

'With the One True God, faith can move mountains,' he cried.

The granite slab hardly budged.

'It seems to have trouble with doors, though,' added Hotfa acidly.

Zhod got his breath back and told Hotfa that she should have wedged the door open.

'Like with the Thief, maybe,' snapped Hotfa, who had been thinking the same way herself.

'Stop bitching,' interjected Slammer. 'That door weighs a ton. No way do we move it, any more than an anaemic gnome could budge a cliff face.'

'Faith can move . . .' began the Cleric, but fell silent at Hotfa's expression. A pause.

'So how do we escape?'

At Slammer's words the statue stirred.

'It talks!' yelled Gripper.

'Hush! Listen!'

'I answer questions, three a day;

Put not your trust in all I say;

If your queries lengthy be

Then I will speak confusingly,' intoned the statue, sepulchrally.

He then rolls to open the door: a 3 suffices; because of his Strength, a roll of 1–5 would do.
The D.M. is prompting the players through an N.P.C.; they should, naturally, have checked the door.

The D.M. has been counting the minute before the door shuts. Not aloud.

The door shuts as the D.M. reaches 60 in his silent count.
The D.M. rules that Slammer, with his exceptional Strength, has a slight chance to force open what is, strictly, a one-way door. He decides arbitrarily that Slammer must roll ((Strength × 2) − 20) on d% (:) a roll of 16 or less. Slammer rolls 37 and fails.
Zhod has a 2% chance of opening the door. He rolls a 12: good, but not good enough.

More advice from the D.M.: retrospective, again, but the players may remember it next time.

The D.M. has been listening carefully for anyone saying 'How'.

'Grotty poetry,' said Hotfa.

Zhod, Slammer and Hotfa went into a huddle.

'Three questions we've got,' said Slammer.

'Nor all correctly answered. Just like a machination of sorcery. I like this ill.'

'Hush, Zhod. It'll probably only lie once,' whispered the Magic-user. 'Don't speak too loud, or you may blow a question.'

'Let's ask "Where is the Sword of the Sorcerer?" That's not too long.'

"Good one. Go.'

Slammer asked the question, but the statue remained silent.

'It's useless,' said Hotfa. 'It's a practical joke.'

'Nay, milady. Let us venture another question ere we despair,' urged the Cleric.

'He's talking bad poetry, now.'

'No, let him try,' said Slammer.

'Would you like to join the One True Faith?' cried the Cleric. The statue did not stir.

'Anyone else want to try?' queried Hotfa.

No one did.

'So, we're trapped,' said Gripper.

'We know,' snapped Hotfa.

'Well, how long will our rations last?' thought Slammer aloud. Hotfa glared at him, but the statue quivered and spoke.

'The rest of your lives.'

'Not very helpful,' said Slammer.

'Hang on,' interjected Hotfa. 'Let's assume it's lying. Then the next two answers are right.'

'Suppose it isn't lying.'

'Then we're in trouble. That's why I'm assuming.'

'Hey,' said Slammer, 'I've sussed it out. Our questions have to begin with . . .'

'Ssh!' yelled the Magic-user. 'I know.'

Their next question was discussed at some length by the three, while Gripper sulked in the corner. At last, Slammer asked the statue:

'How can we leave this room?'

'Through the secret door in the west wall,' replied the monolith.

Zhod ascertained that the statue had told the truth and Slammer and Hotfa debated their next question.

Hotfa is correct, but was unwise to irritate the D.M.
The D.M. rolls the wandering monster die roll, 2 turns having elapsed.
A 4: no wanderers appear.

As the players start to ask questions, the D.M. rolls to see which answer will be false. 1 or 2, the first, 3 or 4, the second, 5 or 6, the third, he decides; a 2 is rolled.

A slight nudge from the D.M.

N.P.C.s are people, too.

The D.M. is unwise to say this as it commits him to what will happen in the future. This is a problem with all oracles and predictions, as the D.M. cannot actually predict the future.

If you know where a secret door is, there is no difficulty in finding it.

'What d'you think of "aitch-oh-double-you do we find the Sword of the Sorcerer?",' whispered the Fighter.

'Natch,' rejoined Hotfa. '"With difficulty", it might say.' But before they could agree on a query for the artifact Gripper butted in.

'How do I get rid of this smell?' he asked.

The others gazed, amazed, as the statue spoke.

'Wash your clothes and your body in water or similar solvent.'

Hotfa was the first to recover. 'You zeeb! That was our last question,' she shouted.

Gripper mumbled defensively. Slammer stepped towards the Thief, checked himself, and asked 'How do we find the Sword of the Sorcerer?' in desperation.

But the statue had fallen silent and would speak no more.

Recriminations over, they left the room through the secret door, which Gripper opened. They followed the passage, the Thief leading the way, until they found a door in the left-hand wall.

'I can't hear anything.'

Slammer kicked the door down and leapt inside. The room was bare.

'Nothing,' he said.

'Why did you kick the door? That was really stupid.'

'Sorry . . . what is this place?'

The room was strange indeed. The walls were adorned with paintings of Halflings being maimed, tortured and molested.

'Sick,' said Slammer.

'Yeah,' added Hotfa. 'Hey Gripper . . . Where is he?'

For the Thief had gone.

'He's going down the passage,' Zhod hissed. 'Come, let us follow him.'

They ran after Gripper as fast as they could without making much noise. The Halfling had heard the sound of rushing water and headed towards it, obviously wishing to wash himself.

Gripper tripped on the first wet step and rolled headlong down the flight of twisting stone stairs. He crashed on to the shingle and lay a moment before crawling into the pool. The others soon came down the stairs, rather more carefully, and found his short sword abandoned on the beach. They blinked to get used to the light.

'Where is he?' whispered Slammer.

'Dunno . . . he must've gone in,' replied Zhod. They could see it

Gripper is role-playing his Intelligence/Wisdom, annoyed at Hotfa's treatment of him.

The D.M. mentions that the sound of rushing water can be heard from down the passage, but only Gripper is interested. He passes a note to the D.M. telling him that he is leaving the party and heading for the water. From now on, Gripper and the D.M. communicate with notes.

Slammer can't hear anything because there is nothing to hear, but the D.M. rolls anyway, so as not to give that fact away.

The room is empty, but still has character. Had the party studied the paintings in detail, the D.M. would have had to invent details off the cuff.

Time for a wandering monster check: a 6, so no monsters.

Normally, a Save versus Dexterity on d20 would be required, but as Gripper is running, the D.M. adds 5 to the roll which comes up 19. Gripper falls and suffers 1–3 damage which results in 1 point's worth of damage. He drops his sword on the beach so as not to get it wet. As the other players state explicitly that they are being careful, the D.M. gives them a subtraction of 5 on their die rolls against slipping. They all roll the required number and so do not fall. This room has natural was a cave, or, more precisely, a collapsed room. A 'hole' in the far wall let in a breeze that stirred Hotfa's hair. She smoothed it back, and muttered to the other two.

'A storeroom once, I reckon: see the barrels? And those fish – they must be feeding on the food that's left. And over . . . look!'

'What is it?' asked Slammer.

'Look, dummy! a pile of fishbones!'

Zhod hefted his mace and peered into the gloom. 'Can't see it: bring the torch closer.'

Slammer was confused. 'See what?'

'Whatever ate the fish. If it gets Gripper, he's in trouble.'

Gripper finished rubbing the murky water all over himself and his clothes and swam to the surface. He gasped for air, coughed, wiped his face with one hand while treading water with the other, and saw the Lizardman reaching down for him.

The others saw it too, and Slammer and Zhod splashed into the water. The Lizardman turned to face them and let go of Gripper, who floundered about in the water, helpless. Slammer swung at the Lizard, but, hampered by the water up to his chest, hit only air. The Lizardman moved back, and Zhod missed as well. The Cleric lifted Gripper to a shallower area of the pool where he could stand and Slammer rushed after the Lizardman. The creature snatched up a sword from behind a rock and turned on the Fighter. Slammer slashed, but the blow bounced off the creature's rubbery hide. The Lizardman swung at the Fighter, who twisted to catch a blow on his well-armoured forearm. To his surprise, the sword bit through the plate armour and into his arm. He lost his footing and fell heavily. As he lay, wondering how to avoid the Lizard's next blow, he heard Hotfa shouting.

'Move, meathead,' she yelled.

Slammer rolled to one side as the sword smashed down where he had been. As the monster lifted the sword, Hotfa chanted and clicked her fingers at it. As Slammer clambered to his feet, the Lizardman stood still.

'Give him the sword, Lizard,' called Hotfa. 'By the handle,' she added, and 'don't kill it, Slammer.'

light and so, for the first round, characters are at a slight disadvantage with a −2 penalty on their combat die rolls.

See the following note.

This kind of deductive logic is always dangerous, because the D.M. may have made a detail up at random. Normally, however, the detail will be relevant, so consider the implications of the contents of the rooms.
The others are accustomed to the light by now.

Around this point the party starts acting as one again instead of passing notes.
The combat begins: in round 1 the party rolls 4 for initiative, the Lizardman 5. He drops Gripper and moves backwards. Slammer attacks and rolls a 7: +3 for his Strength but −2 for the water (D.M.'s decision) makes 8: less than the 14 he needs, so he misses. Zhod rolls 13 modified to 11 and misses too. Round 2: the Lizardman picks up a sword and so automatically loses initiative. Zhod moves to help Gripper. Slammer attacks the Lizardman and rolls 9: modified to 12 (he's out of the water now) which nearly hits. The Lizardman needs 14 to hit Slammer and rolls 13, which hits when the magic sword bonus is taken into account. The damage roll is 2, plus 2 for magic, plus 1 for strength, makes 5 points of damage. The Fighter gets off lightly but has only 2 hit points left, even so. As the rock is wet, the D.M. makes Slammer Save versus Dexterity to keep his footing. He rolls 15 and falls. Round 3: the Lizard man wins initiative, 3 to 2 and rolls a 7, missing Slammer even with the +2. This is a desperate moment for the party, as one more hit will kill Slammer. Hotfa doesn't know that the sword is magic, but still thinks that it is worth using a Charm spell on the Lizardman. The Lizardman needs 16 to Save but rolls 6: he is Charmed and sees Hotfa as his best friend. He accedes, thus, to her request to give Slammer the

'I won't,' he yelled back, sliding the sword into his scabbard and probing his damaged arm with its fellow.

'Hoi, Lizardman,' she continued. 'Any treasure in here?'

The creature grinned and stooped behind the rock. It brought up a bag, leathern, which clinked.

'Show it to Slammer.'

The Fighter took the pouch and poked around in it. 'Five copper,' he shouted back, disgusted, and gave the bag back to the Lizard.

'Come on, let's go,' and Slammer and the Lizard waded through the pool to join the others.

'Do I give him a sword?' asked Slammer.

'Yeah, no hassle. He's charmed, right? He'll stay that way for months, if we don't break the spell. C'mon, Slammer.'

They went up the stairs, the Lizardman in front. Gripper was undamaged, and no longer stank of locust. Zhod wrapped Slammer's arm in a bandage, and the Fighter could use it without too much pain.

'Listen. D'you think this could be . . . the Sword?'

'The Sword?'

'I mean, the Sword of the Sorcerer.'

'Er . . . no. Well, let me look,' said Hotfa.

Hotfa examined the blade minutely. No writings, no runes. Nothing special.

'Reckon not. Why do you think it's magic?'

'Let's have it back. That Lizardman: he wouldn't have mincemeated a fly, normally, but he ketchuped my arm.'

'Well, I can't see anything. Back home I'll use a spell, see if anything shows up.'

'All right. Where now?'

'With your arm like that, we should get back.'

'I can take it: it's not serious. Anyway, we can't get back through the statue room because of the door, unless you want to wait for someone on the other side to open it.' Slammer pointed at the door on the left wall of the passage. 'You think through here?'

'Uh-huh. But we do it properly this time. Thief: listen.'

'Can't hear anything.'

Slammer moved and heaved the door open. They saw a passage stretching ahead for a good twenty feet before turning to the right.

sword, a fairly reasonable demand.

The treasure is as noted in the room description.

Not a good move, as the Lizardman is charmed and won't protest if Slammer robs it, but 5 copper (50 p) are hardly worth it.

Because of the rules, Slammer can fight on as if undamaged while he has a single hit point, but no harm in adding a little realism. A bandage cuts down the risk of disease in any case.

A wandering monster die roll comes up 1. On d6 the result is 5: this means that the wanderers are Kobolds; on a roll of d4 the result indicates that there are three of them. The D.M. names them Fungus, Typhus and Delirius. During the following conversation among the players, he rolls their hit points on a d4: 4, 2 and 2. He waits for a good time for them to appear.

Detect Magic would show if the sword was magic, but not what its properties were. The characters' local sage, the Incomprehensible Bard, would be more specific, but would charge a fee.

The D.M. rolls again, but as before there is nothing to hear.

Slammer stepped through, then Gripper. Hotfa and Lizardman followed and Zhod brought up the rear.

'Wedge the door open, someone,' remembered the Magic-user, but the Fighter interrupted.

'Hey, what's that humming?'

'Humming?' queried Zhod, securing the door.

'He's right: I can hear it now,' corrected Hotfa.

'It's my sword,' said Slammer, pushing his way back past the Halfling to show Hotfa. His eyes widened as he saw the Kobolds behind the Cleric.

'Zhod!' he shouted, and ran to the man of god's aid.

The warning was only just in time. Zhod wheeled to face two Kobolds; a third attacked the Lizardman. Slammer saw a Kobold's shortsword pierce the Cleric's armour and strike home; the other's attack was deflected. He heard the Lizardman roar and wondered whether it, too, was wounded.

The Cleric swiped at a Kobold with his mace and it staggered back at the force of the blow, but returned to the attack. Zhod caught its stroke on his shield. The Lizardman found himself beset by both of the other creatures. One stabbed it in the thigh and was decapitated by the victim's sword. Slammer pushed Zhod out of the way. The Kobolds' attacks went wild, and the Lizard hit only air. The fighter feinted and swung at the left-hand Kobold. The sword twisted in his hands and diced the monster's stomach.

'Did you see that?' shouted Slammer. 'I hamburgered it!'

The other Kobold ran away, unhindered by the Lizardman.

Clear marching order. Helpful for the D.M.
The D.M. decides that the Kobolds have appeared 70 feet to the east, at the corner by the door of Room 22.
The players are learning from their mistakes but might have been better, had they only known, to wedge it shut.
Slammer's sword is humming, because the three Kobolds are now within 20 feet.

When a party meets a monster one or other may be surprised. The Kobolds roll a 4 and the party a 2. Slammer's warning stops the party from being attacked from behind but they are still surprised. The Kobolds get a round's free action before the party recovers. The passage is 10 feet wide and so two characters can fight side by side. Note that the Kobolds, being small, can all fight simultaneously. The Lizardman and the Cleric are at the back so one Kobold attacks each of them. The D.M. rolls a die to see which of the two, the third Kobold will attack. He rolls an odd number so it attacks the Cleric. The Kobolds need a 17 to hit the Cleric and a 14 for the Lizardman. The rolls are 9, 18 and 13 respectively so Fungus has hit the Cleric doing 3, −1 for his pathetic strength, making 2 hit points damage in all. The Lizardman is hit but Typhus's blow bounces off the scaly hide. End of Round 1.

Round 2: The party roll a 6 for initiative, the Kobolds 4. The Cleric needs a 12 to hit, he rolls a 17 and hits Fungus, doing 2 damage. Fungus rolls 16, narrowly missing Zhod, who would have been hit but for his shield. Delirius switches to the Lizardman and rolls a 16, hitting him for 5 damage (6−1 for strength). Typhus rolls 3 and misses. The Lizardman rolls a natural 20 followed by a 5 for damage: Delirius is dead.
Round 3: The Kobolds win initiative and make a morale check, as the third Kobold is dead. They roll 3 on 2d6 easily enough to continue. They roll 5 and 11, though, and miss Zhod. The Lizardman rolled 6 and missed as well. Slammer rolled 17 +3 for Strength +2 for magic sword (not that he knows this) and the Kobold is hit.

Slammer and Zhod rifled the pockets of the two dead beasts, but found little of interest.

'Some copper; fourteen, I make it, a handkerchief. I don't know what this is. A curtain ring, maybe. Magic, Hotfa?' The Fighter flipped it to her.

'Can't tell; I'll wear it anyway. Thanks. What's in there, Zhod?'

'One silver, four copper, and this.'

'Huh.'

'It's a dice, I suppose.'

'Die. Forget it. No, Slammer, I don't think it's magic. The Halfling can have it. Let's move.'

Slammer peered back round the door.

'Has the Kobold gone for its mates, perhaps? I'll look.'

He disappeared round the corner and returned a moment later.

'It's gone, and my sword's stopped humming. No: it's started again.

'Every time you go through a door, it either starts or stops. It's obviously meant to tell you whether you've gone through an odd or even number of doors. How useful. Something worthwhile you've found, Slammer,' said Hotfa sarcastically.

They moved up the passage and, when it turned right, were faced with a choice of doors, one to the right, the other to the left, set in a wall that crossed the corridor obliquely. Gripper listened at the right-hand door, but failed to hear anything. At the left-hand door, he heard muttering, and then a scream that carried even to the rest of the party.

'That was a Halfling screaming!' cried Gripper. 'We must rescue her.'

'No,' said Hotfa emphatically. 'There's obviously something bothering her.'

The damage is an automatic 5 for Strength and magic and Slammer rolls 9: a total of 14 damage. Slammer, for once, understated!

Round 4: The Kobold wins initiative, makes a morale check at +1 on the dice, having seen Fungus's fate: 8 and he runs for the hills. The Lizardman, being charmed, does not pursue him but would have done had Hotfa so requested.

The players announce that they are searching the body. Money is rolled by the D.M.; the curtain ring, handkerchief and die were invented off the cuff by the D.M. to add colour. Had the monsters not been wanderers, treasure would have been written down before-hand.

Perhaps not, as it was a wandering monster; but Slammer was right to think of it. He would have been better, however, to have chased it beforehand.

The Kobold has got far enough away.

The sword starts humming again because of the Bugbear in Room 11.

The D.M. rolls, even though the Bugbear is so quiet it cannot be heard.

At the other door, the D.M. rolls a 2 for Gripper's listening, and tells him what he could hear. The scream is loud enough for everyone to hear.

Alignment is important here. The Lawfuls want to rescue the captive. Gripper is Neutral, but is loyal to the other Halfling. A Human would not necessarily be so quick to put itself at risk. Hotfa is the

'Yes, exactly.'

'I don't want it to bother us.'

There was a babble of protest from the three adventurers and the Lizardman stepped menacingly towards them. Hotfa checked him.

'We've got to go this way to get out, anyway,' put in Slammer. 'That door takes us back the way we came.'

Hotfa capitulated with an ill grace.

'If you want, but we do it my way. Gripper: check the door.'

The Thief's capable hands ran over the door and he shook his

head. Slammer and Zhod moved, one to either side of Gripper, who stepped backwards and said, 'I reckon it's clean.' Zhod mouthed prayers to his god. Slammer kicked once and the door sprang back. Zhod and he were through it almost together.

There were living Skeletons, each with a wicked-looking scimitar,

in the corners of the room. In the far right-hand corner the Fighter glimpsed a tall man in black robes and a waifish Halfling maiden in white. In the middle of the room a pole ran from ceiling to floor. Tied to it by a length of chain was the largest Gecko Slammer had ever seen.

The Skeletons clicked into life and rattled towards the two as the rest of the party came through the door. Gripper loosed off a shot with his shortbow, having sheathed his sword, and hit the black-robed figure. Slammer backed away from the oncoming Undead, but Zhod faced them boldly and, raising his holy symbol, shouted, 'In the name of the One True God, get thee gone, hellspawn! Nay, back, vile creatures! Return to the pits whence ye crawled, wretched abom . . .' The Skeletons hardly paused to cut the old man down, but threw back their skulls in obscene triumph. An unearthly rattle emanated from their deformed throats. The Cleric lay crumpled on the floor, his symbol still clasped in his right hand.

Slammer was frightened now and thought fast. No time for thought, though: the twain Undead were upon him. The third was a good way behind, one of Gripper's arrows nestling between its ribs, grotesque. The Lizardman rushed to join Slammer, and Slammer's sword smashed a Skeleton's skull to flying shards of splintered bone; the thing fell at his feet, a heap of bones no more terrifying than a child's game of spillikins. The Lizardman fared worse; a Skeleton's only character not wishing to go to the resue, but has some pull as leader. The charmed Lizardman will of course protect her. With the others against her, she gives in.

Gripper tells the D.M. he is trying to 'find traps'. The door isn't trapped, but the D.M. rolls secretly anyhow. A 43, so the Thief would not have found any traps. The D.M. tells Gripper that he has found nothing.
Slammer rolls a 2 and opens the door. The surprise roll for Odric is 1, so the occupants are surprised. The party, however, has heard the noises, and so the D.M. does not roll for them.

The party has a round's worth of surprise, and uses it advancing into the room, except for Gripper.
The scimitar is not an official weapon in Basic. For our purposes, it does 1d8 damage. A single-handed weapon, but difficult for the untrained to use.
A Gecko is a large lizard.

Note that Hotfa has shot her bolt, having used the charm spell.

In his round of surprise, Gripper shoots at the evil Cleric. The D.M. tells him that he might hit Rosa, but he trusts in his high Dexterity and fires away. The range is sixty feet, medium for a shortbow, so he needs a 15 to hit. The D.M. rules that 4 or less will hit Rosa, but Gripper has a +3 for Dexterity, so this is unlikely. In the event, Gripper rolls 15, so he hits the Cleric for 2 points of damage.

The Cleric tries to turn the Skeletons, but rolls a 4, missing the 7 he needs. The Skeletons attack, needing 17: they roll 2 and 18. The damage roll is 3, which kills Zhod. Gripper looses off an arrow at the third Skeleton. At short range he gets +1 to hit, with a +3 for Dexterity. 19 hits for 2 damage. The Lizardman, at command from Hotfa, joins Slammer but cannot yet attack. Slammer, lastly, rolls a 14, modified to 19, to hit a Skeleton. He rolls 5 for damage, +5 for shining scimitar slashed his septum. A split second later Slammer's sword struck a second time: another Skeleton was slain. A sudden silence, shattered by the maiden.

Slammer heard her scream and whirled. The Gecko was slavering in anticipation: the black priest was dragging the Halfling girl by the hair towards its waiting jaws. Gripper rushed to save her.

'It's useless,' shouted Slammer. But it was too late. Gripper was joined in a desperate battle for survival. His friends ran to try to save him, for, alone, he could but perish!

Strength and magic, destroying the Skeleton. Slammer, notice, does between 6 and 15 damage with his sword: dangerous were it not for his very low hit points.

Round 3: Odric's group wins initiative. He starts to drag Rosa towards the Gecko. The skeleton attacks the Lizardman and rolls 15 to hit, followed by 2 for damage. Slammer, predictably, pulverizes it with 16 followed by a total of 9 damage.

The third Skeleton is taking a detour to avoid the Gecko. Gripper rushes to try to save Rosa, who has screamed sometime during the party's move.

Round 4: The battle continues . . .

✠ five ✠

The Dungeon Master

The part which the Dungeon Master takes in the adventure itself is very different from that of the players. Acting as he does as information provider and game moderator, he must be careful to ensure that the players and monsters act in the way that they ought to and do not use information that is not available to them. In other words, to run a fair and enjoyable game, the referee must put himself in a similar position to the players and role-play all the various creatures encountered in the course of an adventure. There is one major difference, however, between the players and the D.M., and that is that the D.M. has the power to change anything he sees fit, to a reasonable extent. Should the D.M., for example, realize that his Wandering Monster Table produces results which are likely to annihilate the party, he should feel free to reduce the number of monsters or to change their types. Really major changes in the rules, such as altering the magic system, should wait until the end of an adventure, perhaps be discussed with the players and, at least, be play-tested in a 'pocket-universe', a small area specially created for the purpose.

As a D.M., you may have to play any number of roles: from kind-hearted innkeeper to scheming guide; from paranoid Halfling to fearsome Dragon. Be prepared for all of this, as the interaction with N.P.C.s can prove the most enjoyable and exciting part of an adventure, for the players. The game revolves around the D.M. It is not a straight competition between referee and players, but more a co-operative effort: the more both you and your players put into playing, the more you will obtain from it.

The first session of any campaign is crucial to both the Dungeon Master and the players. If they have never met before, some time will have to be spent on introductions. After this, the process of character generation must be started, so that the players have some characters to adventure in the dungeon. What the D.M. actually brings along to any session is fairly important. All notes should be brought, at least initially. Later on, the D.M. need only bring those notes detailing the areas which the players could possibly reach. The point is that the D.M. should not be caught unaware, if, say, the players leave one dungeon and travel to another. One way to deal with this is to have one folder which contains notes on the particular dungeon or area in which the players are currently adventuring, and another which holds the notes on the other areas which the D.M. has created. In this way, the D.M. can effectively run a game without the necessity of leafing through sheaves of notes to find an appropriate place, or of stopping the game when players leave the dungeon. If figures or other accessories are being used, these also should, naturally, be brought along.

The D.M. should ensure that he can see all the players during the game, so that he can make certain that the players are not cheating in any way, and also so that he can speak to all the players at once. There are few things more detrimental to a game than the D.M. losing the attention of the players, and this can easily happen if they are seated where he cannot easily address them. Similarly, try to avoid having your players involved in games of noughts and crosses, or watching the television, or any of a number of similar distractions. This is not to say that the players should be held at gun-point, merely that their attention should be kept on the game.

Character generation has already been detailed in Chapter 2, but a few additional words are necessary for the D.M. Firstly, it is often a good idea for the D.M. to be present when the rolls for attributes are made. Some over-zealous players are inclined to alter their attributes more than is allowed for in the rules. In the case of novice players, the D.M.'s presence will be necessary if they need the processes explained to them. In addition, advice may be given on which character classes to choose.

It is helpful to have a duplicate character sheet to be kept by the D.M. This enables him, should he so wish, to examine a character's attributes during play without having to take the player's only record of the character. In addition, the D.M. may wish to record certain things on his copy of the character sheet that the player should not know. These might include curses which have been placed on the character, details of magic items which the character owns and so on. It makes it possible to plan the dungeon with the characters' strengths and abilities in mind. An alternative is for the D.M. to take each player's character sheet at the end of the session, ensuring that no unauthorized alterations are made and that no character sheets are lost, unless of course the D.M. loses them all!

When play is actually ready to begin, the D.M. should start by pointing out that, during the adventure, players are only permitted to read sections 1 to 4 (up to, but not including, Giving Experience Points, on page 24) of the Basic rulebook. This ensures that the players do not have a complete run-down on the monsters that they meet. He should also point out any assumptions he is making, such as that characters are right-handed, stand in front of treasure chests they are opening, and so on, unless, of course, the players state otherwise.

The Dungeon Master can now read out some form of background information to the players. He might have prepared sheets of information on commonly available and current knowledge, such as the languages, races and rulers of the immediate area. The information may or may not include the background to the dungeon, as the D.M. may wish to make the characters find out this information for themselves, by speaking to an innkeeper, for example. One good idea is to give different information to each player. Such information might include rumours about what is contained in the dungeon, hints on other dungeons or pieces of general background. This means that players who have a Neutral character might demand payment for their information, or, if Chaotic, may refuse to give it, or not tell the truth. If the players want to write out their own personal background, this is fine, so long as they do not make themselves the favourite son of the Grand Overlord, on a two-year holiday. Examples of personal background can be found in the Introduction. Such backgrounds can be used by the D.M. to work out some later scenarios: for example, Slammer might lead an expedition to take back his farm.

Even if there is no established village for a campaign, with keys and descriptions of inhabitants, it is a good idea to have some form of abstract base, at the very least. Tell characters that they are living in a village, even if this is not described. Generally, they should be living in an inn of some description, which means that they will have to pay something towards their upkeep. As well as this, it is possible to use other customers at the inn as sources of information for the characters and even as possible adversaries. If the D.M. wishes to expand his campaign to include a village, a detailed plan of the inn is not a bad place to start.

At this stage in an adventure, the characters will be ready to enter the dungeon. To facilitate the expansion of a campaign to include wilderness areas, the D.M. should provide a small amount of information on the area between the village and the dungeon entrance. There should generally be no encounters of any significance, except perhaps a passing conversation with a local peasant.

In the cases of the innkeeper, the peasant and the terrain between the village and the dungeon entrance, the D.M. will have to begin the task of describing to the characters what they see and also taking the roles of the various monsters and creatures which have just been met. The most important thing to remember when describing terrain, or dungeon rooms for that matter, is that not everything will be noticed at a superficial glance. Characters who open a door and decide that the six Hobgoblins on the other side are too powerful opposition will not notice details of the tapestry, furniture or, indeed, very much about the room at all. A vague idea of the room size and contents would be all that could be gathered. It is also important to remember that, under the circumstances of lighting in most dungeons, characters will be unable to see much, unless they use some sort of light source. The Basic rulebook guidelines are that a torch or lantern casts light for thirty feet in all directions, so the D.M. should not describe rooms much beyond this thirty-foot radius. If a party has a member with infravision, the D.M. can describe things up to sixty feet away, but only in terms of shape. It is not effective in light, but non-Humans can see normally in this, anyway.

Be careful, when describing something which the characters are examining, not to give away things which they could not possibly know. For example, if the party came across the Sword of the Sorcerer, the D.M. should say, 'You see a double-handed sword. The blade is normal steel and the hilt is set with two blue gems,' rather than, 'You see the Sword of the Sorcerer. It is +2 and emits a low humming when it is within twenty feet of any Chaotic creature.' In this case the players would need the benefit of a Detect Magic spell or perhaps the aid of a sage. Of course, it is not good for the game to keep players guessing too long. After a time they may work out why it hums and that it is magical, but if not, the D.M. should suggest they see a sage. As an alternative, if they know it is magic, tell the particular player whose character owns the sword that the bonus is +2, or whatever.

The first time that players pass through an area of a dungeon, the D.M. should describe the area in detail, but if the characters rush through the area a second time, they are unlikely to notice small changes.

When describing rooms, if it becomes clear that the players are taking little interest in what is being said, either too much irrelevant detail is being included, in which case you should cut it down in future, or the D.M. is failing to make the relevant points exciting; not much can be done about this except to remember that the game is meant to be fun and not just a mental exercise. If a D.M. has made sketches of rooms he can show them to the players, indicating that this is what the characters see on entering the rooms. This will mean that players need not keep asking the D.M. to repeat his description, and they also add vividness to the adventure. If sketches are not available, the D.M. should remember that a room is three-dimensional and not just a plan with key. The D.M.'s description should enable the players to visualize an actual place.

A number of other things should be remembered while running an adventure. One is that it should not be made obvious when something odd is about to happen. If, every time the dice are rolled, the characters duck and the spear trap misses, something is wrong. This can easily be remedied by frequently rolling the dice in a fairly random fashion, perhaps consulting tables for no real reason, and so on. Another solution is to make some rolls in advance and others at the relevant moment. This means that players will always be kept on their toes, not just when the D.M. is seen to be rolling the dice. Another habit which should be encouraged is note-passing between the D.M. and players and between different players. Otherwise, if, for example, the D.M. wishes to inform the player at the back of the party that he has been grabbed from behind, restrained and gagged, it will look suspicious if he passes a note to the player in question.

Again, should a Thief wish to steal from a member of his party, it will look suspicious if he is the only person to have passed a note during the whole of that session. This passing of notes will not slow play unduly, but will allow players to keep secrets from each other and will give the D.M. more opportunities for surprising the players or creating things which affect only one character. If, moreover, the party actually separates into two or more groups, either the groups will have to play at two different times or the parties can be dealt with one at a time, with one party leaving the room and going elsewhere while the other is playing. If this is done, beware of one group of players attempting to spy on another.

The first actual encounter with monsters may come at the entrance to the dungeon, and so it is important to know in what order the characters are moving. This can be done easily if model figures are being used, but if not, the D.M. ought to get the players to write down their marching order. In the case of the Shrine of Kollchap, the adventurers might blunder into the Hobgoblins, and then the D.M. would have to describe the monsters to the players. If this is the party's first adventure, the D.M. should describe the monsters in detail, but mention that they are Hobgoblins. Thereafter he can simply identify them by name only.

The very first encounter with potentially hostile monsters is crucial. The possibilities of combat, negotiation or flight are opened up and the D.M. has to concentrate on what the party is doing, what the monsters are doing and on rolling dice for combat, all at the same time. Naturally, the dungeon key will not give exact details on what any monster will do in each and every situation. The D.M. will, almost certainly, have to ad lib. If, for example, the characters fled the Hobgoblins at the entrance to Kollchap, the D.M. might rule that they ran in the direction of impassable forest. Alternatively, he may make an extra wandering monster appear in the party's path of flight. In this way the D.M. can avoid the party missing the dungeon completely. This is not to say that the party should be channelled into doing certain things; the players should always determine the main part of the story line or plot of an adventure. Only when the party is going right off course, or is in great danger of being killed through no fault of its own, should the D.M. interfere. If, for example, the D.M. has placed clues throughout the dungeon as to the whereabouts of a magic item, the party may simply miss all of these and so end up in a situation where it has explored almost the whole dungeon and cannot ascertain the hiding place of the item. In such a case, the D.M. may, if he feels justified in doing so, place another clue in an area through which the party will soon pass. This should not, of course, be done to reward parties for their bad play, merely to ensure that those who have missed things through sheer bad luck are not overly penalized. Also, if the players constantly fail to achieve their objectives they may become discouraged. The D.M. can make sure that this does not happen by altering the difficulty of his dungeon while play is in progress. D.M.s should feel no compunction when altering die rolls, rules and events if they feel this will improve the game. It is important, however, that the players do not realize that this is being done, as it is just as annoying to feel that what you have achieved is not through your own endeavours as to feel that you have not achieved something which you ought to have done.

Should players make mistakes through their own fault, the D.M. should not, of course, inform them, at least not immediately. The player mapping might make a thirty-foot-square room forty foot square by accident and so eventually the party may reach a situation where their surroundings and their map clearly do not tally. Where a party of adventurers is confused or muddled, as in attempting to find a way out of a complex maze, the D.M. need not step in to help the players if they become somewhat disorientated. If, however, a party spends too much time attempting to work something out, the D.M. should either give them some sort of hint or should distract them by some means, such as a wandering monster.

Most players will try to persuade the D.M. that they have thought of everything. If a player does not have an item of equipment on his character sheet, a D.M. should not allow him to use it. If a character has not stated that he has made a change in where he keeps equipment, such as replacing a dagger in a scabbard, he should be ruled not to have done so. If, however, a character tries to do something which is impossible, for example, opening a door while both hands are full, the D.M. should inform him that something must be put down. Players do not gather treasure if they do not state that they are picking it up. Of course, this should not be taken to extremes: a party would hardly leave without vital equipment such as weapons or backpacks, or if they did they would soon notice the loss. If a character does state that he is doing something that would change his character sheet, such as dropping equipment, the D.M. should note this to prevent arguments later. Indeed, the D.M. should take note of hit points lost and so on.

An allied point is that a D.M. should not presume that characters do something merely because he expects them to. If, for example, the D.M. places a cursed gem in a treasure, but the characters happen to decide among themselves to leave the treasure until their return, the D.M. should not suddenly say, 'When you have walked fifty feet down the passage that gem you picked up suddenly explodes.' As the characters did not say that they had picked up the treasure, the D.M. has made a mistake in assuming that they have done so and the party should not suffer the effects of the exploding gem. The best idea is to take back the statement and say that the gem never existed. This should not be allowed to become a catch-all excuse for parties to escape dangerous situations: if the party had said, 'We pick up the treasure,' the D.M. would be justified in claiming that this included the gem.

During the first adventure, your players may not know exactly what is going on. They may be unsure of rules, and so in situations where an experienced adventurer would easily survive, a novice might not. Gargoyles, for example, can be hit only by magical weapons, and if the party has none, they might advance into certain death. In this case, the D.M. should point out that the party will probably perish, as it is unable to hit the Gargoyles. If they do not know that Green Slime cannot be hurt by any means except fire and cold, the D.M. should say that their weapons are ineffective, but he should not tell them how to kill it. The distinction between these two cases is that in the first instance the party has no means of killing the monsters and should be so warned before attacking, whereas, in the second, the characters do have the capability to destroy Green Slime and so should be left to discover it by trial and error. The players should have been allowed to read all the monster descriptions in the Basic rulebook before starting the adventure, but should not be allowed to refer to them once play has started. Some hints need to be given to the players, but not as many as could be garnered from the rulebook. This applies equally to N.P.C.s: there is little way a character can tell, from looking at an N.P.C., that he is second-level, has 17 Dexterity and speaks Orcish. The players should not be able to play upon the N.P.C.'s precise strengths and weaknesses.

During the D.M.'s first few adventures he will almost certainly make mistakes. Many of these can easily be rectified, such as misunderstanding combat rules or rolling too many hit dice for a monster. In the case of major errors, some difficulty may be faced. If a magic item has been found which is much too powerful (a +4 sword, for example), the D.M. may rule that the item will work only at certain times, from dawn to dusk, say, or only a certain number of times, during twenty combats, for example. Unless something is radically wrong with the dungeon, no really major changes will have to be made.

Do not hesitate to rely on the rules, either. The players will probably forgive your failings, at least at first. Although there is little worse than a D&D campaign which grinds to a halt every few seconds, consulting the rulebook occasionally can save more in playability than it costs in time. Only when you are very experienced will you be able to play without referring to the book, but placing monster statistics and so on in your dungeon key helps to decrease the number of times that reference is necessary. Some play aids, especially Dungeon Master's screens, are designed to aid the D.M. in this respect (see Chapter 6).

Once the players enter the dungeon, they expect a world of mystery and adventure. As no D.M. can have thought of every possibility, it is a good idea to get into the habit of inventing details off the cuff. For example, in the module provided, there is no reference to the moss, or lack of it, on the wall of the entrance tunnel. An inquisitive player might ask if there was any and it would be a simple matter for the D.M. to decide that there was, and that it was yellow and foul-smelling. If players ask about unimportant details, be prepared to ad lib. Especially in the first adventure, do not try to hustle players on into the areas where greater challenges await them. If players appear to be enjoying themselves simply exploring empty passageways, this is fine. In a way, it shows that the D.M. has succeeded in creating an atmosphere, for even empty areas could hold potential danger in the best-planned dungeon. In any case, a well-timed wandering monster will soon hurry on the most dilatory of parties.

Lack of interest, on the other hand, is often caused by the monotony of so-called 'hack-and-slay' adventuring in which adventurers merely progress through rooms, destroying the occupants and amassing treasure. A large number of players dislike this. The D.M. can cater for them by introducing more problem-solving and encouraging negotiation with monsters. In the module given, the players might try to negotiate with Belisarius, the Thief, in Room 5. Since he is hiding and in fear of his life, he might well be a little suspicious at first, but if it became evident that the party meant him no immediate harm, he might join them and offer to act as a guide in return for protection. If, however, the going became difficult, he would probably flee. It is also important to remember that non-intelligent creatures cannot negotiate: Giant Spiders, Rats, Giant Beetles and Killer Bees are all examples of this category. They cannot communicate or understand, and so there is no possibility of negotiation. A D.M. might, however, allow players to get past such obstacles with distractions, such as creating loud noises coming from another direction or throwing food to the monster. If players are ingenious in their inventions, they should be suitably rewarded.

The case of intelligent monsters is very different. Only limited communication is possible if neither side speaks the same language: only signs and hand signals can be made. Rather than having the players say, 'We try to show we mean no harm,' it is a good idea to get them to demonstrate this physically. An alternative is to use a character's attributes as a rough guide as to how well the message is put over. For example, the D.M. might take the character's Wisdom and Intelligence, add them together and double that figure, the result being the percentage chance of success. If the D.M. considers a monster to be especially intelligent or particularly slow-witted, bonuses or penalties can be used to modify this chance. For example, Hotfa tries to get an Ogre she has met to let her through his room, for a fee. She tries a combination of pointing to money pouches and other signals. Her Wisdom is 9 and Intelligence 16, so the D.M. assigns a 50% chance. Hotfa rolls a 37 on d%, meaning that the Ogre understands. Of course, the mere fact of comprehension does not mean that the offer will be accepted. That is another matter and is related to her Charisma. Whenever the D.M. is faced with a similar situation, he can either assign an appropriate percentage to a character's chance of doing something or examine the feat or action more carefully and decide which attributes are important: for example, Strength is relevant to moving a heavy rock. The D.M. can express the attributes, suitably adjusted, as a percentage and allow success if the player rolls that number or less on d%.

In some cases, tables are given, and so the D.M. has no need to work out the chance himself. Chances for opening doors, hearing noise and so on are all provided. In the case of negotiation, the crucial table is the Monster Reaction Table. A dice roll determines the monster's reaction, from immediate attack to enthusiastic friendliness, with something more moderate being likelier. Of course, the two extremes are rare; in the rulebook table they occur on a roll of a 2 or 12 respectively on 2d6. The D.M. may modify the roll as he sees fit, or simply choose the reaction himself. If players offer very large bribes, a bonus of perhaps +1 can be added, or, if monsters are mortal enemies of the characters, they will automatically be hostile. In the Shrine of Kollchap, Odric would be friendly towards the party only for exceptional reasons and would almost always seek to destroy the party if it was in his power. Especially in the case of N.P.C.s, be wary of letting monsters be tricked out of too much. After all, would the average player let his character give away a brand-new +1 axe to an unknown Dwarf? This would be very unlikely, unless, perhaps, the character owed the Dwarf 1,000 gps and had no other means of paying. The D.M. should, in general, play N.P.C.s as people with interests, desires, abilities and fears of their own.

When role-playing monsters, a D.M. should, as a rule, try to keep within their general characteristics and type. When a monster is about to do something really significant, the D.M. should ask himself whether the monster would really do such an action. For example, a solitary Kobold would hardly attack a party of eight adventurers. Intelligent monsters are frequently played by D.M.s as if they were mindless, and this should be avoided. Monsters will sometimes ignore intrusions into their lair if the threat is too great. Intelligent ones will fight reasonably fiercely to safeguard treasure, but not if they face inevitable death.

As well as the monsters placed in rooms, the D.M. should bear in mind that he has the option of using wandering monsters. Rolls are generally made once every two turns to determine if any such monsters appear (a 1 on 1d6 indicating a wanderer). Of course, if players make excessive noise or draw attention to their presence in some other way, rolls should be made more often. Conversely, if the players decide to camp down a dungeon for some while, wandering monster checks should be made less often.

Wanderers appear at a distance of twenty to 120 feet from a party, and so it is worth considering such options as having the monsters come from behind or lurk around passage corners, not just coming from straight ahead. These wandering monsters should not just materialize forty feet down the passage, but should represent monsters moving between rooms. The dungeon key shows what will actually be met in the rooms when the characters enter them, but the dungeon should appear to the players to be an active place and so wandering monster rolls are used. Not all monsters met in a passageway will come under the strict heading of wandering monster; some may be regular planned guard patrols. Similarly if a monster flees combat it may go and inform others of the presence and whereabouts of the intruders. In the case of the Chaotic monsters in Kollchap, however, not too much co-operation could be expected. Run monsters within their alignments, with Lawful creatures being more likely to act out a set pattern and so on.

Should negotiation fail, as it often does, or if it is not attempted, the players may find themselves in combat. In many cases, the chance for surprise exists, but the D.M. should disallow this if the characters have been noisy or if they have been in the room negotiating with the monster beforehand, for example. If neither side is surprised, another roll is made for initiative. In the rules the option of having 'paired' combats is given whereby each character faces one monster or group of monsters and a separate initiative roll is made for each section of the fight. This tends only to work in small melees, as otherwise the number of rolls needed is too great. If figures are not being used, however, paired combat may be helpful, as the D.M. can control whom a character may or may not attack.

The actual mechanics of combat are as important for the player as for the referee and have been dealt with in Chapter 4. Some points, however, concern the D.M. alone. He should not tell characters how many hit points a monster has left although he may, if he wishes, give hints, such as 'The Goblin looks in a pretty bad way'. This should not, on the whole, be extended to characters' hit points as it reduces the players' interest in the game and also gives the D.M. too much bookkeeping to do. In some cases, a combat will be going heavily against the party as a result of bad luck, and the D.M. might intervene; for example, ruling that a monster's attack is a miss, even though the number required for a hit has been rolled. The D.M. might also like to reduce the damage inflicted by monsters. This is possible only if the players cannot see the dice-rolling, and so most rolls should be made in secret by the D.M. Players should, however, be allowed to make their own combat rolls as otherwise their interest may be lost. Such 'fiddling' by the D.M. should be done with care and balance and only in cases where the game might break down without it: when, for example, a group of players has lost an entire party twice in a row and looks likely to lose a third. If, every time a party of adventurers came across a roughly equivalent group of monsters, each side took 50% casualties, the game would soon degenerate. As a rough guide, try to ensure that out of a party of ten to twelve adventurers no more than one or two die in the normal course of an adventure, and out of a party of four most should survive at least four adventures. Remember that the point of the game for the players is enjoyment and the building-up of their characters, and they will get neither of these if the characters continually perish. As always, however, if the party does something patently stupid, let it learn from its mistakes.

An alternative method for ensuring a better rate of character survival is for the D.M. to rule that a character reduced to o hit points or below is simply unconscious. Any further hit will automatically kill the character, but for six rounds the character will live. After six rounds unattended, the character will bleed to death, but if the character's wounds are bound he will recover consciousness six turns later. He will be able to walk, with aid, but cannot carry equipment or wear armour. He will need to convalesce for a fortnight, during which time he cannot take part in any adventures, but then he will have returned to the condition he was in before the battle in which he was critically wounded. This rule reduces the number of deaths and adds a touch of realism, as well as providing the party with the new problem of getting unconscious members out of danger.

As mentioned earlier, creatures will not usually fight against odds that seem hopeless. D&D uses morale rules to cover this. Each monster has a morale rating on a scale from 2 to 12 and when the monster's resolve is in doubt, 2d6 are rolled; if the result is more than its morale, the monster retreats or attempts a fighting withdrawal. Otherwise, it continues fighting. Morale checks are made after a side's first death and when half of its members have been killed or incapacitated. A single monster makes checks when it takes its first wound and when it has lost about half of its hit points. If a monster is winning or losing, an appropriate adjustment is made to the check. Intelligent creatures who fail their morale check may decide not to retreat but to surrender. Some N.P.C.s may have a ransom paid for them; others may tell characters where their treasure is, in return for freedom. Player-characters never have a morale check imposed upon them, but may, of course, decide to surrender. Intelligent monsters will not automatically kill their captives; some may free the characters, having looted them of valuables; others may keep them prisoner, waiting for possible ransom. In the Shrine of Kollchap, prisoners are kept in the cells ready to be sacrificed to the Gecko. In each of these cases the interesting possibility of escape exists. If, on the other hand, characters have tried to flee, a monster, if it thinks itself strong enough, may attempt to pursue the characters. If it is faster than they are, and if they do not take preventative measures such as throwing treasure or food to the monster, it will catch them.

In combat, it is well to remember that certain things which characters try to do are impossible, while others are more difficult than players may claim. Clearly, a character cannot draw his double-handed sword while holding a lantern. A character who tries to creep up on an opponent while invisible (magically possible in D&D) may be heard or even accidentally hit; invisibility does not equal inaudibility or lack of substance. Some characters who are battling with a monster may try to claim that they can help a comrade at the opposite end of the room. The D.M. can easily see whether this is possible if figures and floor plans are being used (see Chapter 6); if not, the D.M. should keep in mind the rough shape and size of the room when players try to have their characters perform such actions.

Running traps and other inanimate parts of the dungeon is much easier than handling encounters with monsters. With most traps it is clear whether or not a character has activated them. Players may try to claim that their character was bending double and so avoided the spear which was intended for his head. As in all such situations, the D.M. should use his judgement to determine what a character's usual action would be, unless, of course, the player had previously specified an unusual course of action. It is important, when dealing with traps, not to move too soon; be sure that a character is moving in a certain way before springing the trap and so on. Some traps rely on substances such as sleep gas; the D.M. should, in such cases, merely inform the players at first that they smell something odd, and only later that they feel drowsy, by which time it may be too late to escape. Others will be swift, and a way of avoiding them might be to poke ahead, perhaps with a pole. Whatever the trap, there should always be an escape. Some traps may not injure a character greatly but merely inconvenience him; falling down a five-foot-deep pit might break flasks of oil rather than bones. Traps are often found by Thieves using their Find Traps ability. Remember to roll in secret to see if a Thief finds a trap, so that the Thief will not know, if he finds no trap, whether this was due to the fact that there was no trap there or that he failed on the die roll.

Doors, and in particular secret doors, rather resemble traps. Firstly, if characters listen at a door and succeed in hearing what is on the other side, the D.M. should not say, 'You hear three Goblins, armed with shields and spears.' At most the D.M. should give away the fact that there were Goblins on the other side, but he would be more likely to describe the sound as 'low rumbling speech'. In general, secret doors should be easy to operate, once found, but some may require levers or buttons to be pulled or pushed and the D.M. may allow experimentation, or perhaps relate success to the character's Intelligence. One special type of trap is poison. The Basic rulebook allows characters a Save against Poison, but suggests that, if they fail, they die. This is very harsh and D.M.s should have poisons in their campaign which do not kill but paralyse, cause immense pain, permanent loss of Constitution or Strength or other non-fatal effects. Players should not be allowed to use poison unless they manage to extract it from a trap or distil it from poisoned stingers, in which case the possibility exists that characters will die in the attempt.

The fact that D&D has a time scale is forgotten by many D.M.s. To move 120 feet takes an unarmoured man a turn, or ten minutes. In this time the Orc-that-got-away could have achieved a lot; he might, for example, be on the way to fetch Odric or the Goblins, in the case of Kollchap. Characters must rest one turn in every six or face a penalty of −1 on all combat rolls until they do. Of course, if parties consistently refuse to rest, these penalties should be increased. Similarly, characters must eat: the D.M. should force players to cross off rations as these are eaten. If these run out, the party will be forced to return to the surface.

You might feel that the movement rates in D&D are rather too slow: 120 feet in ten minutes works out at roughly one mile in seven hours. This, however, allows for the poor lighting in most dungeons, the need to map and time for decision-making. While moving at such a rate, the D.M. should allow players a reasonable amount of time to talk and plan, but in melee rounds of ten seconds apiece he should force players to make swift decisions. One thing which slows down movement is encumbrance. The rules are, in general, good on this point, but there is one problem: that of miscellaneous equipment, which weighs eighty coins-weight no matter how much there is. If a D.M. has time he should break equipment down and work out values for each, comparing them to weapons, and remembering that encumbrance encompasses not only weight, but also bulkiness and difficulty of carrying. A few examples to aid a D.M. in this process are that a lantern should weigh about forty coins and fifty feet of rope about sixty coins. To compensate for this, allow especially strong characters a bonus on the amount which they can carry. For example, characters with 18 Strength might be permitted 800 coins extra weight before becoming overloaded, with 17 Strength 600 coins extra and so on down to 14 Strength, where the normal limit of 1,600 coins applies.

When dealing with characters' abilities and special skills a great deal of care is needed. If Thieves try to hide in shadows or move silently, the D.M. should never tell the player whether or not this was successful. Again, a character trying to hide in shadows in a brilliantly lit room will fail whatever roll the D.M. makes. The D.M. should penalize Thieves attempting to climb especially slippery walls, by perhaps doubling the chance of falling. Abilities such as detecting secret doors and finding passages, traps and shifting walls apply only when a character is actively searching.

Characters should make every attempt to play within their alignment. If a Lawful player consistently butchers helpless prisoners or a Chaotic acts in a set pattern, the D.M. should take action. At first he should inform the player that he is playing outside his alignment, and in most cases this will suffice, as the player will quickly mend his ways. Should he not, the D.M. will force him to change his alignment, probably with some loss of experience points. The D.M. can keep track of alignment either by marking the character's position on a Law–Neutral–Chaos line and moving this mark around after each adventure, depending on the character's actions, or by assigning the character a number on a scale from 1 to 45, with 1–15 representing Chaotic, 16–30 Neutral and 31–45 Lawful, and changing the value appropriately.

There is another, and perhaps more serious, way in which players fail to conform to the personality of their character. This consists of such things as using information which a previous character possessed but which this one does not, or, even worse, communicating such information to other players. The good role-player will not do this and will be content with the character he has rolled. If such problems do arise, however, remind the player that such information is not available. If the player persists, more drastic action is necessary. One interesting idea is to rule that the present character is being possessed by the spirit of the dead one, and so will periodically go into blackouts when the other side of the personality, the dead character, is in control. For these times the character is a N.P.C. under the D.M.'s control. There may be a particular problem in campaigns where there are only a few players and so each has two or more characters. It can be overcome by having the characters separated and meeting rarely, if at all. In some situations, D.M.s allow characters from other people's campaigns to join their own. This is all right as long as the character is not too experienced and does not have overly powerful magic items. If the D.M. tries this way of playing and finds that it does not work, he must simply tell players that they must generate a new character.

In a good campaign Chaotics may work against Lawfuls and vice versa. Elves may dislike Dwarves, both may dislike Halflings and so on. A series of grudges, loves, hates and desires will be built up. In addition, if there is a N.P.C. in the party, the D.M. may use him to stir things up a little. He can also be invaluable to the D.M. as a source of information to the party. He can warn them of monsters that cannot be hit and a host of other things. He should not, however, do the players' work for them and will often suggest things when it is too late. Of course, N.P.C.s will have their own plans and ambitions, and high-level ones may refuse to take orders from the party.

One of the main reasons for adventuring is the pecuniary reward. The D.M. will already have placed the treasures and magic items in his dungeon key and only in the case of wandering monsters will new treasure have to be generated. Wanderers will, in any case, have little or none. In treasure hoards players may find maps, magical items or just ordinary gold, gems and jewellery. Not all treasure hoards are lying on the floor in plain view; one of the most cunning hiding places is in the stomach of the monster itself. Not all magic items operate on demand. Some have command words which must be spoken to activate them. Observant players may hear the monster speaking these words if it uses the item against the party. If not, players will have to guess the word or as a last resort take the items to a sage. Words should, in general, be easy to guess and there might be some clue around.

Apart from treasure, the major reward for adventurers is experience. Players get experience points (XPs) for non-magical treasure recovered from a dungeon and for overcoming monsters by magic, wits or fighting. Experience is also awarded for actions, so that if a Thief picks a pocket he will gain some points. In general, one XP is awarded for each gold piece of treasure gained. Experience for overcoming monsters depends on the power of the creature, ranging from 5 XPs for a Kobold to 1,000 XPs for a Dragon. In addition, bonuses are given for monsters with special abilities such as paralysis. The total of XPs is divided by the number of survivors and this amount awarded to each party member. On average it should take about five successful adventures for all the characters in a party to reach second level, but of course if the players are particularly ingenious they will progress more rapidly. Experience is the best area in which to penalize players not playing their alignment. If, moreover, the D.M. has helped players in a particular encounter, the experience for that encounter should be reduced. In addition, if in the course of an adventure the D.M. considers a player to have shown good sense, then he should award an experience point bonus of perhaps 25% or simply give a lump sum of extra experience points. Poor players can be penalized, but it is always better to reward good play than to penalize bad play.

It can sometimes happen that the D.M. realizes that the rewards given to his characters have been too great, when compared to the risks taken. The simple answer to this is that fewer experience points should be awarded, and also that a very wealthy but not necessarily very powerful group of adventurers would soon attract the attentions of Thieves and other undesirables, not to mention the fact that prices in the inn and shops might start to rise. Do not, however, do anything as drastic as taking the cash away. Never force players into a predetermined course of action, for role-playing is all about the choices players make for their characters, and if a group feels the D.M. is pushing them around too much and relieving them of their treasure as soon as they get it, they will soon become disgruntled.

During the course of an adventure, and indeed when it is over, be prepared to listen to complaints about the way in which you handled this or that situation. If the complaint is justified, and something can be done to rectify it without drastically altering the situation, then do it. Be slightly democratic: it is all very well to run your campaign with an iron fist, but players will soon desert it. When making changes to the rules the D.M. should be moderate. After all, the players have come for a game of D&D, not something dreamed up by the D.M. on the spot. Wherever the rules are lacking, on the other hand, the D.M. should be encouraged to work and create new rules to cover the situation.

If you have great problems with your players, you should be prepared to alter your style of play. A D.M. may veer towards 'realism' and detail at the expense of 'playability' or go in the opposite direction. This is fine as long as his players are happy. If they are not, the D.M. must change his ideas or hand over to another player and become a character-player himself.

If your campaign is successful, new players may wish to join. If they are already experienced in playing D&D there will be little problem: simply add them to the personnel of the next expedition. If new players wish to join who have never played before, they should watch the main group for a time and then, when they get to know the game, join in as player-characters. Experienced players could take the parts of men-at-arms or other hirelings, but new players should always play a full character.

If, for some reason, your campaign cannot continue – if you move away from the area for instance – there is always the possibility of advertising for players in the new area, and this time you will not have to build up your campaign from scratch. If this is not possible, there are always opportunities for postal play and solo dungeons. Although postal D&D can be incredibly slow and boring, a well-managed game can be fairly exciting and many are advertised in magazines (see Chapter 6). A few solo dungeons are commercially available, but it is a simple matter to draw up a series of tables for corridor length, direction, room contents, treasures and monsters and then 'roll' your way a dungeon.

As the D.M. becomes more and more experienced, the possibilities for play open out. He can build more dungeons or expand sections of the rules to include gods, for example, in his campaign. If he progresses to Expert or Advanced D&D, players can climb to levels higher than the third; cities and towns come into play. Large-scale time becomes more important, as events take shape in the outside world; the characters can become great personages in their world; heroes indeed, not the humble treasure-seekers they began as. The Dungeon Master will see characters adventure in his world and see that world unfold, and he can be proud of his achievement.

✠ six ✠

Figures and other accessories

Few games can do without accessories, but few are not improved by them. D&D's main additions are models, modules and magazines. Figures are most likely to appeal to converts from wargaming, who may miss the table-top armies they are used to. With the prices of figures these days, table-top armies, as such, are probably things of the past, but the improvements in the quality of figures mean that one can be proud of individual models, instead of the glitter of armies *en masse*. It was probably never possible to amass armies of the numbers of real ones, anyway: in most rules one figure was meant to represent twenty soldiers, or some similar compromise. It may have been this and other such problems that led to an interest in skirmish games, where one figure was one man, the time-scale was continuous, and so on, an interest that contributed to the success of D&D.

Figures are usually made of lead alloy and come unpainted in a variety of sizes. The most common is 25 mm (theoretically, the distance from the soles of the feet to the top of the head of a six-foot human in this scale), but 54 mm figures are known. As there are more different types of figure available in 25 mm, more people are likely to use this scale and, most importantly, it is the cheapest, so anyone wanting to start a figure collection would be best advised to start here.

The most popular manufacturers of 25 mm figures, according to the 1981 Games Day Poll, were Citadel, Asgard and Ral Partha, in that order. Two other favoured manufacturers are Archive and Chronicle. Obviously, there is little point in us discussing specific figures, as ranges change and (God forbid!) companies go out of business. Judgement of figures is, moreover, a very subjective matter.

What we can do, however, is to offer some useful criteria for assessing figures' relative merits. Figures can be divided, fairly arbitrarily, into two categories: characters and monsters. There is a wide range of characters, except for Halflings, who are overlooked by most manufacturers. As for monsters, the 'tribal', common varieties, such as Orcs or Hobgoblins, are covered extensively with different weapons and stances, as are adventurers, but bigger monsters are not so well catered for. Wyverns, Minotaurs and other large monsters occur only once or twice, if at all, in each manufacturer's range. This is not as inconvenient as it might seem, however, because even if there is a variation in size between two different manufacturers' dragons, they will look 'right' next to anyone's adventurers. Large monsters, moreover, are not found in such large numbers down dungeons and so fewer figures will be required.

The first figures you buy will depend mainly on price and personal taste. If you can, always look at a figure before buying it and not just at a photograph. Thereafter there are three main criteria: price, stance and suitability. Prices change so we can offer little help, but there are large variations (ten pence either side of thirty pence for the average adventurer) between ranges: the most expensive is not necessarily the best. The same figure, however, will almost certainly cost the same at different shops, so there is little point in shopping around. It is a good idea to choose figures with a fairly neutral stance, so that they do not look particularly inappropriate, either when marching down the corridor or in combat. For example, a wild Berserker, madly swinging his axe, may look excellent when fighting, but listening at a door he will appear ridiculous. The third, and possibly the most important, consideration is whether the figure 'feels right'. This includes compatibility with the other figures in your collection, both in size and style.

The next step is to decide what figures you will need. You cannot, evidently, buy a figure for every being in existence or, at the start, for every being in your dungeon. One figure for every character is, of course, essential and an extra representative of every character class will be helpful for N.P.C.s. As well as this, six of some humanoid monster, such as Goblins or Orcs, are needed to represent any groups of such monsters encountered. Orcs will, at a pinch, do for Kobolds, Dwarves, Elves, Hobgoblins, Goblins, Gnolls and so on. One Giant Spider can be used for all the insect-like creatures. If there is a Dragon in your dungeon, get a Dragon figure, despite the expense. Asking players to believe that a Giant Spider is a Dragon is too much! Even this meagre selection costs half as much again as the Basic rulebook, but it has a beneficial effect on play.

Anyone selecting a figure-group of the same kind of monster, incidentally, is normally faced with an unhappy choice. He must opt either for an army of clones, all with the same weapon, in the same posture, or for an ill-assorted ragbag of the same monsters wielding a veritable armoury of weapons. Down a dungeon, creatures are likely to come in groups which wield the same weapon, but not in the serried ranks more appropriate to a military passing-out parade. Even if there are two of the same type ('attacking with sword' and 'with sword', for example), there is seldom a variation of more than two, so that in a row every second creature holds his weapon differently, a sort of 'Space Invaders' effect. Even differences in painting cannot completely hide this problem. The range of adventurers is wide; only a few large monsters will appear, and so the problem will be less marked, but with weakish beings appearing in large numbers, the problem is very marked.

There are two solutions, neither completely satisfactory. The first, rather drastic, one is conversion: the angle at which an arm is being carried can be altered by carefully bending it or, better, cutting or filing away part of the figure and re-attaching it, a technique which will be familiar to those who have converted or animated historical military figures. It should not be done by novices without some practice on, for example, plastic figures, as a decapitated model has few uses and is a waste of a good figure. Save any botched jobs, though, as the very occasional severed head adds a good deal of atmosphere to dungeon corridors, cupboards and other out-of-the-way areas.

The other solution is to use a set of 'personalized' figures. Some manufacturers, notably Citadel, vary heads and equipment for their figures, so that each one has some amount of variation while retaining the same weapon. No radically different postures, even so, but it is cheaper than hacking away with a modelling knife.

The D.M. need not buy all the figures, of course; his players can be expected to buy figures for their own characters, at least, and most will want to acquire a more substantial collection.

The simplest function of figures is the representation of marching order. If figures are being used, the D.M. can see at a glance who is likely to be hit by arrows or caught in traps, for example. All these figures look very lonely if they are used only to show marching order, so most D.M.s use them for melee as well. This means monsters are needed but, to start with, the monsters can be doubled up, as detailed above. The rooms and passages can be represented by chalk lines on the table, but dungeon floorplans are probably nicer. These are robust cardboard sheets, coloured to look like a dungeon floor, whether it be flagstone, wood or dirt. A grid is superimposed upon this, so that distances can be determined at a glance. Games Workshop produce some good professional ones, if you can afford them, but cardboard and pencil can be used to make an acceptable substitute. This use of figures prevents any doubt as to where characters are in a melee, and adds greatly to the feel of combat now that players can 'see' the situation rather than having to visualize it. If a Thief wishes to hide in shadows, he can see where the shadows are; a party which wants to surround a monster can tell how much space is available. Similarly, if a trap drops a stone block from the ceiling on to the party, there can be no doubt as to who is underneath. The D.M. will not actually drop a stone block on the models, but may, if he revels in that sort of thing, have a stone block with plasticine adventurers' remains on the underside which he can place in the room and which surviving characters may, if they so desire, try to lift. If models were not in use, some players might suddenly remember that they were lagging behind and thus not under the juggernaut at all. The D.M. could get round this by asking players where they were in the room before he told them of the stone block, but this would alert them to the fact that something was about to happen. In this and similar situations, the use of figures can save endless argument, as long as the D.M. is in the habit of insisting that players' figures move when their characters do.

Figures can be used as soldiers in table-top battles, probably with specific fantasy miniatures rules, such as T.S.R.'s excellent *Swords and Spells*, now, sadly, out of print, but this is outside the scope of this book. If you wish to try table-top gaming, Asgard's *Reaper* and the Skytrex *Middle Earth* rules are both good starting points. Few, if any, role-playing combat systems can be used for army combat without getting bogged down in paperwork.

Painting figures is a near-essential. It is, obviously, a matter of taste exactly how this is done, but some general advice is in order, for complete novices. A cheap brush is not a good economy: it will fall apart sooner than a good one, may moult on to figures while they are being painted, and will do less good work than a proper brush, generally, just as a worn or damaged stylus will leave its mark on a record collection. Two rather more expensive brushes, an oo and a 1, for example, will last a long while and suffice for all the painting necessary, except for large areas of dragon, maybe. Paints are, again, a matter of taste, but you would probably be best with enamels. Humbrol or Airfix are both fine, the former rather better, and any ex-aircraft modeller (or tank, ship or even train modeller, for that matter) will have some paints left. The vital colours are white for undercoating and black for bases (but not the undersides), for both of which matt enamel should be used, even if the rest of the figure is being painted in oils or acrylics. When the figure is painted (and for detailed advice on this, we advise you to look at Shaun Fuller's article 'The Magic Brush', reprinted in *Best of White Dwarf*), you can varnish it, if you wish, though you might prefer to touch up the paint occasionally rather than have a brightly shining figure. Many games of D&D are played by artificial light, so this will show up particularly badly. Using matt varnish is a compromise, and not a particularly effective one, as it is never very matt and also fails to protect the figures. Some care in handling figures will also protect their paint coats, but while players will be careful with their own models, they may, in the heat of the moment, damage other people's!

There are other ways of getting figures than buying commercial metal ones. If your talents lie in that direction, you can sculpt your own figures, mould them and cast them in lead. Most people's lie elsewhere.

Other materials can be used. Plaster is another popular material for do-it-yourself figures, but is better used for dungeon walls, rubble (if the bricks break when you are casting them) and other decor. Plastic figures would be cheaper and more durable than metal ones, but, unfortunately, none are made. Airfix used to make useful Robin

Hood and Sheriff of Nottingham sets in 20 mm scale – compatible, if you were pushed, with 25 mm, and they made perfect Kobolds. Unfortunately they are now out of production. Atlantic make some Greeks, Romans and Egyptians, but in 20 mm (or 54 mm), again.

The other material used for figures is, surprisingly, cardboard. Such figures are available from two or three commercial sources. While they are ready-painted, as it were, they are only two-dimensional and lack the spectacle of solid figures; they tend, moreover, to be fairly expensive for what you get. A list of manufacturers for this type of model is given on p. 169.

No sort of model, it should be emphasized, is necessary for the game, but well-painted figures, in apt settings, and even the use of the tables and chairs that some companies provide, go a long way towards the suspension of disbelief necessary for D&D, and so some can achieve status in their own right, as desirable *objets d'art*. For many players, they add limitlessly to their enjoyment.

There is a myriad of miscellany for D&D. Dice, other than the Dragon Dice provided with boxed Basic, are available; if you prefer d6s to have pips, or if you want different-coloured polyhedrals or even 'gem dice', these can be bought. As a guide, one die will cost about as much as a figure (but d6s should cost *much* less), so consider how many you will really need before buying them. For the decadent, there is even a 'dice maze' to enliven rolling, costing little short of the Basic and Expert rulebooks together.

Other common accessories are referee's shields, discussed briefly in Chapter 1. Their function is to hide the D.M.'s notes from his players and give him all necessary charts at a glance. The only D&D shield, however, is for Advanced D&D, not Basic, and is useless for the second function. The D.M. can make his own, easily and cheaply, from card, with the necessary tables written on it. These are Combat, Saving Throws, Clerical Turning and maybe Wandering Monsters. T.S.R. will probably release a Basic Shield: they already exist for other role-playing games such as *Traveller*, *Boot Hill* and *Gamma World*, further discussion of which is to be found in Chapter 9.

One other miscellaneous accessory that the D.M. may find useful is a calculator, if his mental arithmetic is not all that it might be. A simple one will suffice, without complex mathematical functions like sine or log; even square roots are seldom used, except for distances.

Anything that a calculator cannot handle quickly should have been worked out beforehand. This kind of complication has no real place in the game, anyway. For those this way inclined, Chapter 7 discusses the use of computers in D&D.

A module is a pre-packaged dungeon complete with background, maps, monsters, traps and treasure. The D.M. can use the module immediately, without any work, but of course it lacks the personal touch that home-designed dungeons have. There are three modules designed by T.S.R. for use with Basic D&D, called B1, B2 and B3. It is difficult to say much about these modules without spoiling them for anyone who intends to buy them, but each has specific features which help to introduce both the D.M. and players to the game.

B1, *In Search of the Unknown*, is specifically designed to be relatively easy, and not as hard as a normal module for experienced players. From the players' point of view, it is the same as any other module but slightly easier both in terms of monsters and mapping, since the majority of rooms are rectangular. The module is designed to allow the D.M. some personal involvement: the monsters and treasure are left for him to fill in; the other room details are given.

B2, *The Keep on the Borderlands*, is more conventional, with all monsters and room descriptions completed by T.S.R. There is more emphasis on arriving at the dungeon, as an introduction to wilderness campaigns.

B3, *Palace of the Silver Princess*, has an excellent feature, a short introductory adventure. In this, the D.M. simply reads out a number of alternatives and the players choose one of these, which leads to another selection from several choices. This continues until the party has succeeded in adventuring beyond a certain point, when a normal dungeon style is resumed. This programmed adventure gives a flavour of the proper game, but, since the players cannot do anything unforeseen, the novice D.M. will not be caught out. Combat, however, is left to the players and the D.M.

T.S.R. also produce a number of modules for Advanced D&D (see Chapter 8), but these need not concern the beginning D.M. There are, however, some T.S.R. modules which are designed for use with the Expert rules but which extend the Basic rules, and these are of some value to the Basic D.M. There are two such Expert modules at present: X1, *Isle of Dread*, and X2, *Castle Amber*.

Other companies produce modules, but most of these tend to be aimed at more advanced levels of play. Judges Guild, however, market a number which are approved for use with Basic D&D. These include the *Caverns of Thracia*, a standard dungeon, and *Mines of Custalcon*, a wilderness adventure. *Survival of the Fittest* is a D&D solo dungeon, but can also be played by up to four players, without a referee. Another of their Basic modules, *Temple of Ra*, has special rules for introducing figures.

Dungeon Geomorphs are a compromise between modules and dungeons which the D.M. designs. Unfortunately, they suffer from the failings of both, and have few good features. They are dungeon maps, which can be cut about and rearranged, but have no room descriptions. The intention is to save the D.M. time, but mapping out a dungeon is not a very time-consuming activity anyway. Their drawbacks are that they cost as much as a full module and restrict the creativity of the D.M.

Magazines fall into two categories: professional magazines and amateur ones, known as fanzines. Most are published either in Britain or in the U.S.A. only, and take some time (two months, at least) to cross the Atlantic. Information about role-playing games does not normally date that quickly, but reviews of 'new' products may not be topical by the time you read them. New games have to cross the Atlantic, too, remember.

White Dwarf is Britain's professional, forty-page, magazine. But, although the cover used to advertise a 'game and miniatures magazine', coverage of miniatures is very perfunctory; while most new games are reviewed, there are at most two or three photographs of figures in the 'news' section. Games coverage is good, though. There are always one or two articles concerning D&D and usually a mini-dungeon. Two departments are also devoted to the game: the 'Fiend Factory', which consists of suggestions for new monsters sent in by readers, and 'Treasure Chest', which is devoted to readers' ideas for D&D. Other regular features are 'Starbase', dealing with *Traveller*, 'RuneRites', dealing with *RuneQuest* (but also relevant to D&D), 'Open Box', a usually impartial review of Science Fiction and Fantasy games, and a letters column, which has been the forum for some vigorous philosophical debate. At the moment the magazine is published once every two months, but it should go monthly during

1982. For British D&D players, it is easily the best magazine on the market. Some back issues are still available, but most are out of print. The best parts are, however, preserved in *The Best of White Dwarf*, one volume for scenarios and one for articles. Included in the latter is Don Turnbull's Monstermark system, still the best system for assessing monsters' relative deadliness, and some excellent advice to Dungeon Masters from Lew Pulsipher. Two new character classes, the Houri and the Barbarian, both by Brian Asbury, are introduced. The best ten monsters from the Fiend Factory, and the best selections of Treasure Chest, such as Spells, Magic Items and Traps, also appear. 'The Magic Brush', Shaun Fuller's definitive articles on figure painting as an art, are reproduced there. In the scenarios volume there are several well-thought-out-mini-dungeons, including contributions from many famous D&D personalities. Both these volumes come with the *Best of White Dwarf* advertisements as well, but are still well worth an investigation.

The Dragon is T.S.R.'s magazine. Printed in America, it is more expensive than *White Dwarf*, but contains more, especially more fiction. Its contents are similar in subject matter, although T.S.R.'s non-role-playing games do receive attention, too. D&D, obviously, is the main focus of interest, despite the fact that other companies' systems are discussed. A regular column, 'The Electric Eye', is concerned with micro-computers, a subject that *White Dwarf* might devote space to in the future. *The Dragon*, too, has collected its best articles together and published them in *Best of the Dragon*, I and II.

Military Modelling now incorporates *Battle*, which was a wargaming magazine. The letters column, accordingly, is full of letters from model builders resenting the wargamers' intrusion into 'their' magazine and from historical wargamers attacking the Science Fiction/Fantasy gamers. The magazine itself is largely free from this sort of cliquishness, but is also free of any mention of role-playing games of any description, whereas *Battle* used to run the occasional article. This may be because Charles Vasey, who runs 'Across the Board', a regular column on boardgames, finds role-playing games 'the most simplistic, inane and mundane games on the market'. New products are reviewed quite comprehensively in Wargames Briefing, but there are magazines devoted to wargaming, let alone Science Fiction/Fantasy gaming, which are more useful, such as *Ares*.

S.P.I. produced *Ares* as a bi-monthly magazine, with a game in each issue. The magazine was quite a glossy affair. It had regular reviews of new films and television, which few other gaming magazines offer, and of books, some rather idiosyncratic game reviews and fiction. Two information columns, 'Facts for Fantasy' and 'Science for Science-Fiction', each edited by a Ph.D., displayed the magazine's ancestry. The games were the main features of *Ares*, and divided fairly evenly between Science Fiction and Fantasy subjects, with the former edging slightly ahead in recent issues. The games themselves were never less than playable; some were very good but underrated (*WorldKiller* and *Barbarian Kings*, for example) and the *Pandora* games have already become classic, especially *Voyage*, whose paragraph system has cropped up in a variety of inappropriate places, in game suggestions in 'Feedback'. Apart from S.P.I.'s tendency to foist combat systems from their role-playing games on *Ares*' readers, the games did not, on the whole, seem to have been cobbled together to meet a deadline. As of Issue 9, the rules came separately printed and bound, which was very welcome, as it stopped the magazine from falling apart when the rules were prised out of the centre. (S.P.I. is now defunct, but their games are still available in the shops and probably will be for some time.)

Of the fiction, only Harry Harrison's 'The Return of the Stainless Steel Rat' was by a major writer, but other stories, particularly Ian McDowell's 'Chichevache', and 'The Whispering Mirror', by Richard Lyon and Andrew Offutt, were well worth the reading. None of the fiction, moreover, is spectacularly bad, which it sometimes is in fanzines. The *Ares* management had a policy of attracting the best fiction, and it seemed to be working.

Ares was also the house magazine for *DragonQuest* (another role-playing game described in Chapter 9, as are the other games mentioned below). Game Designers' Workshop publish *The Journal of the Traveller's Aid Society*, devoted exclusively to *Traveller*; *Tunnels and Trolls* has *Sorcerer's Apprentice*, many of whose articles would be of interest to D&D players. *RuneQuest* has *Different Worlds*; *Chivalry and Sorcery* has no professional magazine devoted to it, but *White Dwarf* carries the occasional scenario or article. As far as coverage goes, *Dungeons and Dragons* is by far the most written-about role-playing game, with even *Traveller* and *RuneQuest* trailing far behind.

Gary Gygax says that 'nothing will spoil a campaign as quickly as some of the material offered in the various gaming magazines'. This is doubtless true, and more so of the fanzines than the professionals. Some of the monsters and magic items proposed in these are extremely powerful, and a D.M. would do well to pause and consider before adding any of these to his game. The Fiend Factory in *White Dwarf* gives a 'monstermark' for all its new monsters, which gives some idea of how powerful its creations are, but some of the new magic items or character classes could overbalance a game just as quickly. If a D.M. wishes to test out a new idea he would do well to use it in a 'pocket universe' first, and then, perhaps, include it in a continuing campaign.

There exists a multiplicity of fanzines, but, for the record, the three strongest contestants in the 1981 Games Day Poll were *The Beholder*, *DragonLords* and *The Stormlord*. In any of these you have to take the rough with the smooth, and there is usually a lot of rough. More to the point is that none of the fanzines are particularly cheap, or much longer than a professional magazine of higher-quality content and presentation. Fanzines, obviously, ensure a free press and a forum for rebels (or the editors' friends) to speak out, but the prices they must charge to keep publishing are likely to prohibit anyone from reading more than one or two magazines. The more the merrier, it might be argued, but those who pay the same amount to read a 'zine with one or two good articles as they would pay to read one full of good ones would disagree. Fewer publications might improve quality, because all the good articles would tend to accumulate in the remaining fanzines. Bear in mind the scarcity of good articles when you rush your own 'BeastieButcher' to the presses.

A fairly comprehensive list of magazine publishers can be found at the end of the book.

✠ seven ✠

Computers

While D&D was in its infancy, computers were reaching adolescence. Over the last few years, computing has undergone a revolution, and one which is still continuing. Space Invaders machines are just a visible product of this. That computers should become associated with games, and used for them, was in some ways inevitable: games are, to a certain extent, to do with how well you handle information, and information-handling is what computers are primarily concerned with. No matter how it has come about, there is no doubt that many D&D players are interested in computing (and vice versa); it is not surprising, then, that attempts have been made to computerize the game. As the information technology era continues, other similar attempts will, doubtless, be made.

Before we look at these, it might be a good idea to define exactly what a computer consists of. The essential ingredients are the central processing unit; some way of getting information to it (a keyboard, for example, being the usual method); and some way of getting a reply (a printer, or a screen, known as VDU for visual display unit).

The CPU has a series of instructions, known as a programme, fed into it, and executes this programme. The results that are produced by this are usually displayed by one of the output devices.

It should, then, be possible to play D&D with the computer acting as D.M. (not as a player, for reasons which become obvious when you think how a computer would go about analysing a statement like 'You are in a ten-foot-wide passage . . .'). In practice, though, there are constraints placed upon the computer's role, primarily due to limitation of time and space: space because, even today, it takes a large, powerful (and expensive) machine to store a book the size of the Advanced rules, let alone understand it, and time because even if you did have space for a complex programme it would be unbearably slow. If you have typed 'Open Door', you do not want to wait half-an-hour for the computer to print out 'THE DOOR OPENS'. A computer can store far more than a human, and can do complex or tedious calculations almost infinitely quicker, but it still has limitations. This is, of course, only valid for today's technology: second-guessing progress, especially in this field, is never wise. A far more serious problem is that a computer is, as Harry Harrison said, 'a machine with zero imagination'. A player can come up with more responses to situations than the computer can deal with. The usual solution is to present the player with a 'menu' of alternatives, thus:

    1: GO NORTH
    2: OPEN DOOR
    3: SEARCH ROOM
    4: USE WAND
    WHAT IS YOUR CHOICE?

and so on. The trouble with this is twofold: it gives the player some none-too-subtle hints as to what he should do (using the wand, maybe, in this example) as well as preventing him or her from doing something else (for example, anyone wanting to call for help in this case would be unable to). The second problem is that once you have worked out how to get through the dungeon, it does not change: you are stuck solving a problem you have already solved.

Where a computer does come into its own is in performing tedious tasks that hold the game up. If you think that character generation takes too long, a short programme will produce randomly generated characters as near instantly as makes no difference, the only disadvantage being that you need to admit to yourself how much you normally fiddle the rolls. A computer will also take care of endurance or experience, or maybe even melee if it is not too complicated, and is also very useful as a pocket calculator if you are not good at mental arithmetic: there is a lot of calculation in D&D.

It has been suggested that the computer could store details of monsters, so that the D.M. could find their characteristics without having to flip through the *Monster Manual* and the *Fiend Folio*. There are about 400 monsters in these two books, so a binary chop search would go through at most ten operations to locate a given monster, which would not be unbearably slow. Once the players have got over the initial excitement of seeing the D.M. use a computer, this could speed play considerably, if the D.M. is not in the habit of writing down a monster's statistics when he plots it, which, to be honest, he should be.

The game proper apart, there are a number of computer games similar to D&D, without its complexity. 'Adventure' programmes, and their variants, understand simple English phrases, so that, faced with 'TO THE NORTH IS A HOVEL WITH AN OAKEN DOOR' you can type 'Open Door' and be understood. This alleviates the first part of the 'menu' problem, discussed above, but not the second. If you come up with an idea that the programmer did not think of like 'Listen At Door', you get 'YOU CAN'T DO THAT' or some similarly irritating message. These games tend, also, to be mere problem-solving exercises, interesting enough for hardcore computer freaks, but leaving us ex-wargamers longing for a bit of cold steel and some random violence. When you meet a crocodile and realize that the only way to get past it is to retrace your steps for half-an-hour, pick up the armadillo, find your way back to the crocodile and distract it by feeding it the armadillo, I, for one, would prefer to whip out my trusty sword and dispatch the monster while it slept. The other disadvantage, which goes hand-in-hand with this, is that when you have solved the problems the particular adventure becomes useless and you need another one: they are not cheap, either.

More fun, for those who like a small amount of 'hack-and-slay' between the problem-solving, are the real-time programmes like *Rescue at Rigel*. In this, the player has to rescue hostages scattered around the complex at Rigel, all the while shooting 'tollahs', which come in 'lower' and 'higher' forms: the scenario's derivation is obvious. Down the right-hand side of the screen is a display of the characters' status, rather like a simplified self-updating character record sheet. The rest of the screen is occupied by a graphical display of what is happening to the character. To move, for example, you get your marker facing in the appropriate direction and hit a different key to move forward. Combat is handled similarly. The number of options is, therefore, fairly limited, but the scenario is tightly defined, and the range of objectives with it, so there is no need to do anything not covered by the instruction menu. The game takes place, moreover, in 'real-time'. If a monster is moving towards you, it carries on while you wonder whether to turn 'amble' off: this adds a good deal of tension, as well as frustration for watchers, all of whom see the 'obvious' thing to do while the player fumbles for the correct key!

Rescue is a science fiction game, but the same company makes fantasy games such as *Temple of Apshai, Morloc Tower* and *Datestones of Ryn* and so on, if you want a game that is enjoyable in its own right, rather than a re-creation of D&D. While they lack the imagination of the best D.M.s, and their ability to think on their feet, they are much better than a bad D.M. For the isolated player, computer and solo dungeons are a lifesaver.

Computers have come a long way since the vacuum-tube days of the 1950s and they have a long way to go, both in terms of availability and of power. One thing that is certain, however, is that a lot of software is and will continue to be available dealing with Fantasy-related subjects if not with D&D itself. Lots of people (Gary Gygax, for example) look forward to the day when games are played in real-time with 3-D graphics and so on, and the picture on the screen is what the character is actually seeing. What lies in the future, only time will tell.

✠ eight ✠

Further complexity

The Basic rulebook is extremely limited in its scope. Once a player-character reaches the fourth level, there is no information provided on his abilities or powers. At this point, the D.M. must make a decision: he can restrict his adventurers to the first three levels, forcing those advancing beyond this to retire; he can invent rules to cover the situation; or he can purchase either the Expert Dungeons and Dragons rulebook, which deals with levels from fourth to fourteenth, or the Advanced Dungeons and Dragons Rules System. It should be understood that, although both the Expert and Advanced sets of rules come under the general heading of Dungeons and Dragons, they are different in several major aspects. The Expert D&D rules are, essentially, designed to expand the Basic rulebook. The rules are wholly compatible with those in Basic D&D, and there is little difficulty in progressing from one to another; it is really a matter of mastering the new forms of adventure, abilities of higher levels, and a host of new spells, magic items, equipment and monsters. Advanced Dungeons and Dragons, on the other hand, was not designed with the present Basic set specifically in mind; it was released some two to three years earlier. Some of the obvious differences include the sheer length of the rules – three books with a total of over 250,000 words – and the fact that non-Human races are allowed to have character classes, in the same way as Humans, so that Halfling Thieves, for example, can exist. As well as this, new character classes and sub-classes and races are introduced, together with an expanded alignment system.

For the D.M. who is considering which of the two to progress to after he has exhausted the possibilities of the Basic rules, a few words may help. The Expert rules begin where the Basic rulebook leaves off. They include an assortment of new monsters, many of them more powerful than those of Basic D&D. Characters can pit themselves against Hellhounds, Mummies and Storm Giants (which have fifteen hit dice!). A plethora of new magic items is introduced, some of them of very great power indeed, such as Rings of Three Wishes. In addition, there are rules which deal with character advancement up to the fourteenth level, together with treatment of wilderness, naval and aerial adventures.

One of the helpful aspects of the Expert D&D rulebook is the inclusion of a section on how to use the rules if you have the earlier edition of Basic D&D first published in 1977 (revised in 1978, it came into its present form in 1981). The first edition of Basic was different in some respects from the present rulebook, hence the necessity for a section dealing with it. This means that those D.M.s who are, perhaps, more experienced, but have decided to use the Basic rules with a new set of players, can advance to the Expert rules, even though their Basic set is somewhat out-of-date. The Expert book itself is organized in much the same way as Basic D&D, with an additional section dealing with waterborne adventures. The Introduction suggests that each section of the Expert rulebook could be removed and placed in a ring folder next to the corresponding section of the Basic rulebook. If the rules are properly understood, however, there is probably no need to dismember them.

From the start of Expert D&D, it is made clear that the major innovation in the rulebook is the introduction of wilderness adventures. These take place above ground, in such environments as deserts, hills, badlands and wastelands, which are rarely inhabited by civilized folk, but are populated by all sorts of fearsome monsters. The D.M. must draw up a map of a portion of the world and situate cities, town and creatures on it. A section, which corresponds to the dungeon-design section of the Basic rulebook, gives advice on how to construct a wilderness. A sample, the Grand Duchy of Karameikos, is shown. Some advice is given to the D.M. about wildernesses, such as the caution not to have characters existing in a vacuum with events going on elsewhere, although 'it is important not to force the action to a pre-determined conclusion. The plot lines can always be adjusted for the actions of the players.' This piece of advice would have been better placed in the Basic rulebook, as D.M.s should make some attempt at turning their dungeons into 'living' places, rather than static areas where monsters dwell in rooms and await their inevitable fate.

In general, the transition between simple dungeon adventuring and the wider world is best handled gradually, and the Basic/Expert system allows for this, increased complexity being introduced as the D.M. becomes more experienced. New equipment is detailed which might be of use in the wilderness environment. River boats, wagons, carts and even war galleys are introduced. Rules are given for movement in the wilderness, getting lost, travelling by air, and encounters with monsters. These latter appear to be the main events of any day, apart from the characters losing their way. This tends to produce an atmosphere similar to a dungeon with nothing but wandering monsters, and a D.M. should spice up his wilderness with abandoned ruins, lairs, villages and other features which characters can explore. This does tend to prolong journeys, but is more exciting than a mere 'O.K., you meet a Manticore' for each and every day of travel.

The Base Movement Rates for wilderness adventures are triple those in a dungeon, so that an unarmoured character may move 120 feet in a ten-minute period. The problem comes with the Movement Per Day Table. This shows that the number of miles a character may move per day is one fifth of his movement rate in yards, so that an unarmoured man with no treasure moves 120/5 (=24) miles per day. If, however, the movement rate of 120 feet per turn is used to work out how long it takes to cover 24 miles, the figure of just over 54 hours is obtained. Either Expert D&D postulates very long days or something is wrong. It can be remedied by multiplying the movement rates in the wilderness by five, so that a Base Movement Rate of 120 yards per turn becomes 600 yards. This gives a speed of about 3 miles per hour for an unarmoured character with no treasure, which appears to be reasonable, assuming between eight and ten hours per day are spent actually walking. The D.M. may, of course, wish to take the movement rates as they stand, or alter them in some other fashion.

Among the new features is the Evasion Table, which allows for the possibility of characters wishing to avoid contact with monsters they have encountered in the wilderness. In Basic D&D, this is simply a function of the relative speeds of the monsters and party, fast-moving parties being able to outdistance slow monsters, and vice versa. Rules are also given for combat in the air (on winged creatures such as Pegasi or Hippogriffs, or through magic means such as flying carpets or levitation) or at sea (in war galleys, canoes, merchantmen, etc.).

As the Expert rules cover levels from fourth to fourteenth it is, of course, necessary to include monsters which are capable of standing up to such characters. About a hundred are introduced. Some of these can be used in small numbers to oppose low-level characters, but many, such as the Bronze Golem (20 H.D.; does 3–30 damage on hitting), should be reserved for higher-level parties. Together with new monsters, Expert D&D also introduces new magic items, some one hundred in all. These vastly increase the range, scope and use of magic, and also the danger of the D.M. unbalancing the game by handing out too many. The increase in magic items is not an excuse to scatter them in almost every dungeon room. One interesting feature of these rules is that magic swords now have the possibility of being Intelligent, having alignment, being able to speak and having magical powers such as being able to detect sloping passages, heal wounds or see invisible objects.

The expansion of the levels to include those from fourth to fourteenth necessitates several pages to explain the new powers and abilities of the character classes. It is in the Expert rules that some of the real disadvantages of being non-Human show. Dwarves are only allowed to reach a maximum of twelfth level, Elves may only reach tenth level and Halflings are restricted to the eighth level. Clerics are able to turn Higher Undead, such as Wraiths, Mummies, Spectres and Vampires at high enough level. They can, moreover, 'Dispel' (destroy) some or all of the monsters, if they are sufficiently powerful in comparison to them. Magic-users, Elves and Clerics are able to cast more spells and of greater power, ranging right up to the powerful Animate Dead, Walls of Fire and Reincarnation spells. Thieves have increased chances to open locks, move silently and so on.

When creatures reach ninth level (or eighth in the case of Halflings) they are ruled to have reached 'Name' level: Wizard for Magic-users, Lord for Fighters, Patriarch for Clerics, Master Thief for Thieves, Sheriff for Halflings, Wizard-Lord for Elves and Dwarven Lord for Dwarves. At this level, characters are permitted to settle down and build some sort of base for themselves. Thieves may build hideouts, such as fortified houses or cave networks, and attract two to twelve first-level Thieves as followers. They may then try to set up a Thieves' guild. Other Humans may build castles. Fighters, if they settle down in this way, become Barons; Magic-users gain apprentices, and Clerics obtain from fifty to three hundred fanatically loyal troops. Dwarves, Elves and Halflings may only build 'strongholds'. Dwarves may set up a clan in cave complexes, Elves build in forests and befriend the animals there, while Halflings will build in rolling hills and start a community called a shire. This all has the effect of bringing the characters more into the political life of the world they are in, if, indeed, they are not involved already. Some D.M.s prefer not to have any form of political system which involves the players, and, in this case, these strongholds will have use only as bases in which to store up reserves, recuperate and defend against attackers.

Among the other things included in Expert D&D are details on specialists and mercenaries which may be hired by player/characters. If the party wishes to hire an Alchemist, Animal Tamer, Sage, Engineer or any of a number of other professionals, rules are given for the cost and abilities of the specialist. Armourers, for example, cost 100 gp/month and one is needed for every fifty fighters hired. Armourers not employed in the upkeep of troops can produce one suit of armour, three shields and five weapons each month.

Naturally, the combat and saving throw tables have been expanded to include the new character levels. As well as the Wandering Monster Tables, which have been extended to include Dungeon Levels 4 to 7, Wilderness Encounter Tables have been included to aid the D.M. in his running of such adventures.

In contrast to the Expert rulebook, which adds to what has been laid down in the Basic rulebook without substantially changing any of it, the Advanced rulebook introduces a somewhat different way of playing D&D. It starts off by presenting a high level of complexity, with complete rules on wilderness adventures, town adventures and levels up to about the thirtieth. It is possible to start playing Dungeons and Dragons with the Advanced rulebook, but for the beginner this poses almost insuperable problems. The sheer length of the rules guarantees that most will give up reading before reaching the end. The rules are divided into three books, the *Monster Manual*, which gives descriptions of over 350 monsters, the *Players' Handbook*, which contains information on character generation, spells and adventures for players, and the *Dungeon Master's Guide*, which contains much matter of use to the D.M. such as magic items, combat tables and advice on dungeon design. One so-called benefit of this system is that players are never certain about all the rules about such things as magic items. This does, however, often place a beginner at a serious disadvantage, although it does mean that a player need only read the *Players' Handbook*.

Some of the differences between Advanced D&D and Basic/Expert D&D become apparent from the very start, during the character-generation process. A number of 'sub-classes' are introduced in the former, which are, in effect, variations on the major character classes (Fighter, Cleric, Magic-user and Thief). The sub-classes of Fighter are Paladins and Rangers. Paladins are Fighters dedicated to the cause of Law and Good. They are restricted to actions which are Lawful and Good, and must have fairly high attributes. If they perform Evil or Chaotic deeds, they lose their Paladinhood and skills, which include the detection of evil, making all saving throws at +3 and the ability to cure disease a few times each week. At high levels, Paladins have clerical spells and may turn Undead creatures as Clerics do. Rangers are Fighters who are trained in the arts of woodcraft, tracking, scouting, infiltration and spying. They gain bonuses when attacking Giant-class creatures. They surprise opponents more easily, can track creatures and gain limited spell abilities. On the other hand, they may not hire men-at-arms or other retainers until eighth level, must always remain of a Good alignment and may own only as much as they can carry.

Druids are a sub-class of Clerics dedicated to the preservation of nature. Their spells are more to do with living and growing things, and, in general, affect only animals such as apes and rats, rather than magical creatures such as Dragons. Illusionists are a sub-class of Magic-user whose spells deal with the arts of deception, confusion and trickery. Assassins are a sub-class of Thieves, whose major function is the killing of Humans and other intelligent life forms. Rules are given for assassination, the ability to disguise, make poison and the like. They are able to use many more weapons than Thieves, but are restricted in other thievish abilities.

The Monk is a wholly new character class, not a sub-class of Cleric as might be thought. Monks do not have spells as such. They are 'aesthetics' not, as might be expected, 'ascetics', and they train rigorously to improve their physical and mental talents. They attack with 'Open Hands' in a manner similar to a martial arts adept. As they reach high levels, their armour class becomes better, owing to the ability to dodge, their movement becomes greater, and the damage done by their open-hand attacks increases. Monks also do more damage than normal with ordinary weapons, owing to their knowledge of weapons and anatomy. They are less likely to be surprised, and have certain thievish abilities along with abilities unique to their class: at third level, a Monk can speak with animals and with each level up to the thirteenth he gains a new ability, including the ability to speak with plants, to heal damage on his own body and ultimately to use the deadly 'quivering palm', which enables the Monk to kill a person by setting up deadly vibrations in his body. Restrictions include the fact that Monks have no spells, cannot wear armour or use a shield, do not gain bonuses to hit due to Strength, and may only retain sufficient money for modest up-keep.

In addition to new classes, there are also a number of new races in AD&D. These are Gnomes, Half-Orcs and Half-Elves. Gnomes are smaller cousins of Dwarves, living in underground earthen burrows or rocky hill formations. They are similar in appearance, but are brown in colour and they often have a special relationship with burrowing animals living near them. Half-Elves are crosses between Humans and Elves, having much the same characteristics as Elves, but to a lesser extent. Half-Orcs are the product of cross-breeding between Orcs (ugly human-like creatures which look like a combination of animal and man) and Humans. They are, to quote the rulebook, 'rude, crude, crass and generally obnoxious. Because most are cowardly, they tend to be bullies and cruel to the weak, but they will quickly knuckle under to the stronger.' The races which occur in Basic D&D have slightly different abilities in Advanced. Dwarves can detect traps and determine approximate depth underground, in addition to their other abilities. Elves are 90% resistant to 'Sleep' and 'Charm' spells and are able to detect secret and concealed doors fairly easily. Most important, however, is the separation of race and class so that each character has both. Halflings are no longer mere second-rate Fighters with few advantages. In AD&D they may be Fighters or Thieves. Elves may be Fighters, Magic-users, Thieves or

Assassins and so on. In addition, non-Humans may choose to have a combination of classes: for example, Elves might be Magic-user/ Thieves. Each race, however, is restricted as to which classes and combinations may be chosen, and if a character chooses to be a multi-class he will advance more slowly, as experience is split equally between the two classes.

Whereas Basic D&D has a comparatively simple alignment system – characters being either Lawful, Neutral or Chaotic – Advanced D&D adds an extra dimension, that of Good/Evil. This system may be envisioned as a noughts-and-crosses board with the top row being Good, the bottom row being Evil, the left-hand column being Lawful, the right-hand column being Chaotic and the central row and column appropriately Neutral. Thus, for example, the bottom right-hand corner is Chaotic Evil.

There are many more spells in AD&D. Compared to the eight first-level Cleric spells in Basic D&D there are twelve in AD&D; and as against the twelve fourth-level Magic-user spells in Expert D&D there are twenty-four in Advanced. A spell is set out with its name, type (such as Evocation or Necromantic), level, range, duration, area of effect, components, casting time and saving throw, if any, followed by the explanation/description. It should be noted that, whereas in Basic D&D spells take little time to cast, they are handled differently in AD&D. The round is sub-divided into ten segments, each of six seconds, and the spells are given casting times. In addition, many AD&D spells require material components which must be available for the Magic-user to cast the spell.

The amount of equipment available to adventurers is much larger than in Expert D&D. The selection of weapons is increased, partly by the addition of such obscure arms as Fauchard Forks, Becs de Corbis, Guisarmes, Lochaber Axes, Bohemian Earspoons and Holy Water Sprinklers. Prices are also given for pigs, ponies and songbirds, among other things.

As each character class in AD&D receives a different amount of money to begin with, it is difficult to comment on the relative value of equipment. An average Fighter has 125 gold pieces to begin with, while he receives only 105 gold pieces in Basic. The cost of weapons and armour, however, differs between Basic and Advanced, the latter being generally, but not always, more expensive. The cost of a short sword in Basic is 7 gps; in Advanced it is 8 gps. Plate mail sets a character back 60 gps in Basic but 400 gps in Advanced. The cost of a week's standard rations is 5 gps in Basic and 3 gps in Advanced. In general, perhaps, the major difference between the two systems is that in Basic a first-level Fighter will be able to afford plate mail immediately, whereas in Advanced he will have to wait quite some time for it. In fact, AD&D has many more categories of armour than Basic. One small but irritating difference between the two systems is that an unarmoured man in the Basic/Expert system is A C 9, whereas in Advanced he is A C 10.

As has been previously mentioned, one of the major differences between Expert and Advanced Dungeons and Dragons is the length of the Advanced rules. This is to cater for the many additional sections in AD&D. To mention but a few, the *Players' Handbook* has sections justifying its hit point system and more lengthy discussion of time, distance and movement, as well as Retainers, in AD&D divided into Hirelings (servants, guards, blacksmiths and other trades) and Henchmen (more or less devoted followers of a character). There are over 400 magic items in the *Dungeon Master's Guide* and over 350 monsters in the *Monster Manual*. Although the Advanced rules do include more, they are not arranged as well as the Basic/Expert system. The weights of various items of equipment are given only in the *Dungeon Master's Guide*, whereas they would have been much more suitably placed in the *Players' Handbook*. The mass of detail in the former almost guarantees that much of it will never be used. There is much advice given, but the beginning D.M. will almost certainly get lost, as little attempt is made to distinguish the wood from the trees.

The *Dungeon Master's Guide* claims to include everything vital to the running of the game. Even if this is not so, the amount of material presented is enough to ensure that most situations, if not covered, are at least mentioned: disease, character abilities, upper-level character followers, Thief abilities, spying and Assassins' use of poison are all detailed and explained in the first few pages. Differences that might be noted by the D.M. transferring from Basic to Advanced range from the trivial, such as the slightly different movement rate out-of-doors, to the significant, such as the structuring of melee rounds into ten segments, which can determine what time spells are cast in a round and whether a spell is ruined by the Magic-user being hit. Another important difference is the morale system using a Base 50%

chance, with modifiers if the creature is wounded, its friends desert or it inflicts casualties on the opposing party.

Rules are included for attacks with two weapons and for weapon-less combat. There are separate combat tables for each character class with the result that Thieves and Magic-users are less likely to hit than in Basic, Fighters slightly more likely, and Clerics about the same as before. This means that combat in AD&D is very much more complicated: the description is not clear in places, but an example given clarifies a few points. The beginner to AD&D would do well to spend some time working through the combat rules.

The result is a game in which the D.M. must do more spadework before beginning, but has many more opportunities presented to him. A D.M. who has mastered the Advanced rulebooks will meet few situations which are not covered, fewer certainly than if he had read only Basic/Expert D&D. For example, the *Dungeon Master's Guide* includes a section on random dungeon generation. This can be used by the D.M. to help create a dungeon and it also opens up the possibilities for solo play, as a group of several adventurers control-led by one player can progress through the dungeon while it is being rolled up. When a door is opened, rolls will be made for what is on the other side: if a room, its size, shape, number of exits and contents; if a passage, its width and direction. A section on 'Psionics' in the *Players' Handbook* allows for the inclusion of characters with strange mental powers, such as Telepathy, Mind Control and the abilities to heal wounds or manipulate materials at a distance. In addition, should the D.M. find that he has exhausted the possibilities of the monsters in the *Monster Manual*, with his players getting to know the details of each creature too well, the AD&D rule system contains the *Fiend Folio* which adds almost two hundred monsters, each described in the same way as those in the *Monster Manual*. A further AD&D book is *Deities and Demi-gods*, which gives descriptions of gods from seventeen different pantheons: some historical, such as the Egyptian or Greek, some deriving from Fantasy authors, Fritz Leiber's Nehwon or the Melniboné of Michael Moorcock for example. Included with these are some new rules to cover the use of gods and their relations with their Clerics, but the book is essentially an attempt to put gods into a form usable in AD&D.

The AD&D rulebooks are long and more than a little expensive, each costing roughly twice the price of Basic or Expert D&D. Their arrangement often leaves a lot to be desired, as, in certain places, important rules are swamped by a mass of detail. The artwork and presentation are, on the whole, good, while the amount of information presented makes it admirable if not perfect in every respect. They are suitable for those D.M.s who wish to concentrate on running a rule system rather than a game. Those who wish to ad lib and make up rules on the spot may find that they are discarding a great deal. There is also a slight problem when progressing from Basic to Advanced, in that, although both are essentially the same game, there are several areas of contradiction.

Expert D&D is a much more compact system: much has been cut out and many points clarified. The rules are better set out and are much easier to learn. The artwork is perhaps not so good, but, at the price, Expert D&D has much to offer. As it follows on from Basic D&D, it is ideally suited to the D.M. who does not wish to subject his players to any 'culture shock' as the rules change.

All things considered, it is up to the individual which of the two he chooses. Expert is more highly polished; Advanced contains more, but while it is more commonly played, its expense may deter the average player. Either adds greatly to the excitement and enjoyability of a Dungeons and Dragons campaign.

✝ nine ✝

Other worlds

Soon after D&D's first appearance in 1974, it became obvious that, although the fundamental idea behind the rules, the role-playing concept, was a good one, the game mechanics themselves left much to be desired. The rules failed to cover large areas and were in some places contradictory. Many people realized that there was great potential for similar products with comprehensible and better organized rules. *Tunnels and Trolls*, published by Flying Buffalo Inc. (1975), tried to achieve this by a process of simplification tending towards a more playable, if less realistic, game. *Chivlary and Sorcery*, from Fantasy Games Unlimited (1977), moved in the other direction, towards realism at the expense of playability and added elaborate rules where previously there had only been omissions and ambiguities. At about the same time as *Chivalry and Sorcery* appeared in the Fantasy field, the first Science Fiction role-playing games emerged, heralded by *Metamorphosis Alpha* (1976), but *Traveller*, from Game Designers' Workshop (1977), soon took over the lead in Science Fiction and is still the most popular role-playing game after D&D. *Traveller* was perhaps the first of these games to depart at all significantly from the basic structure of D&D.

Empire of the Petal Throne clearly derives many of its game mechanics from D&D, but the background fantasy world is extremely interesting and well thought out. The game comes with three attractive full-colour maps, one depicting the city of Jakalla, where most adventurers start out, the other two covering the whole of the known portions of the world of Te'kumel. *RuneQuest*, published by the Chaosium in August 1978, also has a very detailed world,

Glorantha, derived from the same company's boardgame *White Bear and Red Moon* (1976), now re-released as *Dragon Pass*. Metagaming Concept's role-playing system *The Fantasy Trip* grew out of *Melee*, a man-to-man combat system, and *Wizard*, a game of magical duelling. For this reason, the emphasis is upon play and the workings of the rules, as opposed to social and historical background. One of the latest games, but already very popular, is S.P.I.'s *DragonQuest*, published in 1980. Learning from the mistakes of other games, S.P.I. have once again created a game worthy of serious attention in the classic Fantasy role-playing mould of D&D.

In the area of Science Fiction there have been, to date, fewer role-playing games. *Gamma World*, by T.S.R., was an early example, appearing in 1978, shortly after *Traveller*. Like many T.S.R. games it was, to a large extent, modelled on D&D, and also drew heavily on T.S.R.'s early venture in the Science Fiction field, *Metamorphosis Alpha*. One excellent innovation, however, is the set of charts dealing with players' attempts to divine the nature of an unknown artifact. The game postulates a world in which a nuclear holocaust has devastated much of civilization. Included is a map of the North American continent with certain geographical features altered, and the referee is also at liberty to add any terrain which he desires. Players play the roles of normal (pure-strain) humans, mutated humans or mutant animals. *Starships and Spacemen*, from Fantasy Games Unlimited, has less emphasis on realism and more on playability than other games from F.G.U. The hardware and setting of the game owe more than a little to the popular TV series *Star Trek*. The *Starship* rules are excellent, but the game has, perhaps, less to offer the veteran role-player, who might be better advised to try *Traveller* or *Space Opera*, also from Fantasy Games Unlimited. *Space Opera*, unsurprisingly, is a complex system, drawing on the experience of *Traveller* and other early S.F. games but still remaining very much an original product. It is probably the most detailed system available and in this and other respects comparisons with *Chivalry and Sorcery* are not unjustified. Some of the worst excesses have been toned down, but it is still not a game that the average player can easily master.

Universe is S.P.I.'s latest role-playing game and is roughly analogous to *DragonQuest* in scope. Like *DragonQuest*, it uses a board and pieces for combat. Unlike most other Science Fiction games, it has proper rules for robots and their use. It also has an excellent three-tier world-generation system whereby the referee can create worlds in as much or as little detail as is appropriate. For example, if the characters merely cruise past the planet in their starship, only broad generalizations about size, atmosphere and gravity need be generated. If they intend to settle down and raise children, every detail must be included, whereas if they only land and refuel the intermediate level of detail will prove adequate. Only time will tell whether *Universe* will encroach upon a market already dominated by *Traveller*.

As has been seen, then, the vast majority of role-playing games deal with Fantasy and Science Fiction subjects. As works in these fields have proliferated, however, occasional forays have been made into other genres. An early example was *Boot Hill*, a T.S.R. game dealing with the Wild West. Unlike many role-playing games from T.S.R., it is for the most part free from the influence of D&D. On the other hand, *Top Secret* (T.S.R., 1980), a game of espionage and adventure reminiscent of the James Bond films, suffers particularly badly from this: the idea of agents being sent out to buy their own equipment, for example, or the fact that the players' notes for the introductory module virtually duplicate the equivalent advice for B1, one of the Basic D&D introductory modules, with 'Human Target' substituted for 'Monster'. It also has slightly irritating names for the levels such as Shoplifter, Mechanic and Torpedo. These minor criticisms apart, *Top Secret* is a highly enjoyable game and a sadly underrated one. The similarities with D&D might be a bonus for those who wish to transfer from D&D to *Top Secret* or vice versa.

A game concerned with a similar subject is *Gangster!* from F.G.U. It deals with crime and law enforcement in prohibition-era America, although the rules can be extended to apply to periods up to the present day. One nice feature is that the more esoteric weapons, such as machine-guns, are not always immediately available on demand, if at all, to the average player-character. Also on the law enforcement theme, albeit from a slightly different angle, are *Villains and Vigilantes* (F.G.U.) and *Superhero 2044* (Gamescience). Both these games deal with superheroes. In the former the character generation by the referee assigning attributes based on his judgement of the players' real strength, intelligence etc. can cause more than a little ill-feeling. While the background is patchy, the list of superhero

powers is extensive and comprehensive. *Superhero 2044* is somewhat more conventional, with attributes being assigned by the
player. An interesting comment on life as the designer sees it is that
the more successful a character is at stamping out crime the less help
he receives from informers. Other non-standard games include *Skull
and Crossbones* (F.G.U.), a game of piracy in the Caribbean, and
Bunnies and Burrows (F.G.U.), a game of intelligent rabbits.

Perhaps the only role-playing game which can claim to be completely divorced from D&D is *En Garde!* (Game Designers' Workshop, 1975). As the title might suggest, this is concerned with
duelling and social climbing in seventeenth-century France. The
combat rules are for one-to-one duelling, with only six types of
weapon permitted. Combat routines such as Lunge, Slash and Parry
are plotted on paper beforehand and put into effect simultaneously.
The aim of the game is to increase your social status and thus join the
élite of society. There need be no referee: players write down beforehand what action they will perform during any given week, such as
visiting a club, joining a regiment or paying court to their mistress.

An example might run like this. Henri and Louis are two captains,
one in the King's Musketeers and the other in the Cardinal's Guard.
Colette is the young lady whose affections are being sought by our
two heroes.

1642 April

	Louis	Henri
Week 1	Visit Blue Gables Club – Carouse	Practise with Rapier
Week 2	As Week 1	Visit Hunters Club – Carouse
Week 3	Court Colette (fails)	Practise with Rapier
Week 4	Court Colette	Court Colette

In the first week Louis visits his club and drinks. He gains status for
being a member of the club and for being seen drinking, although
both of these activities cost him money. He loses 800 crowns on the
gambling tables, but gains status for spending so conspicuously.
Henri, meanwhile, has been practising with his sword and increasing
his expertise. In Week Two they both visit their clubs. Louis loses
300 crowns while Henri wins almost 500. In Week Three Louis

attempts to woo Colette: he spends 84 crowns on gifts and flowers but is rejected (rolls a 2 on the Courting Table!). Henri is again practising hard with his rapier. During the final week Louis returns to Colette's doorstep, laden with roses. Who should he find there but Henri? Neither will step down in favour of the other, naturally enough, for they are members of rival regiments. In the ensuing duel Henri's practice pays off and Louis is badly injured. *Hélas!* As can be seen, *En Garde!* is radically different from Dungeons and Dragons and several features, such as the concept of social status, might make an interesting addition to a D&D campaign.

Throughout the broad spectrum of role-playing games there are certain recurrent themes which are handled differently by the various games. The most important of these are the character-generation system, the background, the combat system and, lastly, the objective or method of progression. As luck would have it, Gygax and Arneson, in Original D&D, came up with a system for generating attributes that produced results with a distribution roughly analogous to that of real life. *Tunnels and Trolls* also uses 3d6 but introduces Luck as an attribute, one almost unique to this game (used for saving throws, combat and the like). Most games, indeed, use this or a similar dice-rolling system for generating characters. *RuneQuest* and *En Garde!* use 3d6; *Traveller* uses 2d6; *Chivalry and Sorcery* uses 1d20; *Boot Hill* and *Top Secret* use 1d100, but with a modification which makes low scores higher by addition on a sliding scale. The attributes used in each particular game are, on the other hand, in most cases different from D&D and a few games make some characteristics interdependent. In *Chivalry and Sorcery*, for example, a low Constitution will set a maximum for a character's Strength. *Chivalry and Sorcery* also has certain attributes, such as Charisma, which are calculated from other characteristics already rolled, in this case Intelligence, Wisdom, Appearance, Bardic Voice and Dexterity. *The Fantasy Trip* moved away from the idea of determining attributes randomly and instead had the player allocate a set number of points between characteristics with certain minima. *DragonQuest* uses a similar system with a preliminary roll to decide the exact number available. If a high number of points is obtained, these must be spread fairly evenly, while if a low number is rolled, the player has the option of placing a large portion of them on one or two characteristics.

In most games, after perhaps a roll or two for hit dice and the like, the player takes over the character and luck plays no further part in its generation. In *Traveller*, however, the attribute rolls are only the beginning. A character must now join a profession of his choice. In the basic three books this can be Army, Navy, Scouts, Marines, Merchants or 'the Others' – which last represents a variety of undefined civilian occupations. A further supplement delineates many of the last category, including Babarians, Belters (Asteroid Miners), Rogues and Bureaucrats. A character signs on for four-year terms of service. Each term the character must roll more than a certain number to avoid being killed in line of duty, and then, if successful, roll to see if he has been promoted. This done, the character receives a certain number of skills, the general area of which is chosen by the player, the exact nature being determined by a roll of the die. At the end of a term a character must make a re-enlistment roll. This decides whether a character must leave the service, may leave the service or, exceptionally, must rejoin. At the end of his career in a particular service a character musters out, receiving a variety of benefits both in material terms and some improvement in characteristics and skills. *Traveller* books 4 and 5, later additions to the original rules, elaborate even on this system, terms being broken down into one-year assignments. This process is enjoyable in its own right and adds greater depth and attachment to the character. One minor problem is that characters have the annoying tendency to die after a fair amount of time has been invested in their creation. An interesting feature is that many characters start out middle-aged, in contrast to most other role-playing systems, where the practice is for adventurers to begin at about the age of 18, or the equivalent if non-Human.

Settings for role-playing games fall into three main categories: Fantasy, Science Fiction and Historical. D&D has essentially a loosely-defined Fantasy setting. There is no attempt to aid or restrict the D.M. by providing a minutely detailed system complete with socio-political, religious, economic and geographical information. In Basic D&D, almost the only help given to the D.M. consists of the list of monsters and hints which can be gleaned from the character classes, although Expert and Advanced D&D are more extensive. The general feel given, though, is of a quasi-medieval nature. All of this is also true of *DragonQuest* and *Tunnels and Trolls*. *Chivalry and Sorcery*, however, is based more strictly on a medieval society.

An attempt is actually made to re-create the social structure of a country during the high Middle Ages. Players are assigned a social background, and this will, to a large extent, determine their outlook on life. The life of a Knight is somewhat different from that of a lowly peasant!

Two games stand out from the rest of the Fantasy field as far as background is concerned: *RuneQuest* and *Empire of the Petal Throne*. The former, as has been previously mentioned, has its origins in the boardgame *White Bear and Red Moon*, and Greg Stafford's fantasy world, Glorantha, is richly imaginative and highly developed. Many of the monsters are completely original, such as the Dragonewts, Scorpionmen and Broos. The amount of detail given allows the referee to concentrate more on the particular scenario rather than expending precious time and effort on establishing the setting. Glorantha, indeed, provides a welcome rest from the all too familiar worlds of D&D, *DragonQuest* and *Tunnels and Trolls*. *Empire of the Petal Throne*'s world Te'kumel is set in the far future, but is a fantasy setting as civilization has degenerated, after a cataclysm, into near barbarism. Metal is extremely scarce, tough animal hides being used for weapons and armour. Even so, there remain some vestiges of the old technology, in the form of various 'eyes' or artifacts with powers which the people of the new Te'kumel regard as magical. At the beginning of the rulebook there is a very extensive exposition of Te'kumel's history and society. Although the dominant race is humanity, there are a number of excellently conceived monsters, some the descendants of starfaring alien races, some originally native to the planet. It is a pity that T.S.R. were unable to find a market for such a fine product, but perhaps it will achieve wider acclaim under its new owners, Gamescience. Its lack of success may be attributed to the fact that some referees find a pre-packaged world overly restrictive, although *RuneQuest*, which could be said to suffer from the same complaint, has proved widely popular.

In most Science Fiction games, of course, the Universe is your oyster, rather than just one world. The background, accordingly, is one level more abstract, positing a civilization spanning the stars. With all the various social systems of history to choose from, S.F. game designers always seem to plump for a loose confederation of worlds with a central government, in which players are free agents (rather like Harry Harrison's universe in the *Deathworld* or *Stainless*

Steel Rat series). This is the system used in *Traveller*, *Space Opera*, *Universe* (just about) and *Starships and Spacemen*. In the latter, player characters are forcibly members of the Federation (dry) Navy, fighting on its behalf against the alien races that infest the galaxy. A lot of constraints are placed on the players by this; in combat, if they retreat before a certain point, they are later court-martialled, and if they fail to retreat with wounds at a given level, the same fate befalls them. This ensures that characters cannot 'beam up' at the first hint of trouble, but is a rather obvious 'game effect device'. Interestingly enough, *Star Trek* had the same problem in many of its episodes, and was sometimes hard put to it to 'trap' the Enterprise crew on a planet.

In the other games, players are civilians adventuring on the 'edge of known space', or wherever – a situation analogous to D&D in space, which is a criticism often levelled at Science Fiction role-playing games. *Traveller*'s planets are graded green, amber and red, for safe, dangerous and no-go worlds. The amber planets do not have the full law-enforcement apparatus of the Imperium, and it is to these, accordingly, that players gravitate. The use of the omnipresent but not always omnipotent Imperium prevents characters getting caught up in galaxy-wide wars while allowing scope for them to indulge in the skulduggery common to Fantasy role-playing but rare, presumably, in the technologically advanced society of most Science Fiction/Fantasy role-playing games. In *Traveller*, oddly, the weapons are all common today, such as pistols, revolvers and rifles, apart from the two laser weapons, but Brian Asbury added some excellent new firearms in an article in *White Dwarf* 11: *Mercenary*, the fourth *Traveller* book, extends the hardware range as far as the Meson Accelerator, which atomizes an area of fifty metres radius. All these weapons are rather powerful.

A sub-set of Science Fiction role-playing games arises from 'After the Holocaust' settings, where Civilization-As-We-Know-It has been devastated by some catastrophe. *Gamma World* used a nuclear war, as did *Aftermath* and *The Morrow Project*. *Metamorphosis Alpha*, by contrast, was set in a spaceship which passed through a cloud of radiation. Radiation in these games is used as a catch-all excuse for mutated animals, to be used as monsters: D&D in space again.

The historical games, naturally, have a predefined background, but not all choose to mention it. *Boot Hill*'s map can be used as either Texas, the Mexican border or Colorado, depending on which way up it is (!), but the game assumes some familiarity with the Western ethos. On the whole most of these games have obvious settings.

The third feature common to all role-playing games is some sort of combat system. Here the dichotomy is between a fast-moving system and a detailed realistic one. D&D opts for the former, and its combat system is simplistic, with one die roll to determine whether a blow hits and another to calculate damage, if necessary. Surprisingly, armour makes a character harder to hit instead of subtracting from the damage. The explanation given is that misses include hits that do not penetrate the armour. The two combatants strike alternately and any damage done is taken from the body as a whole in the form of hit points. Some systems, including *Traveller* and *Chivalry and Sorcery*, are essentially the same, but most game designers realized that it would be more logical for armour to subtract from damage instead of making the wearer harder to hit. *Tunnels and Trolls* was the first game to use this method, but other games added other innovations, especially hit location and critical hits. Hit location specifies the area wounded by legs, arms etc., and a critical hit is one which has an unexpectedly serious result. Such wounds should, obviously, be rare occurrences. Most games achieve this, but, unfortunately, *DragonQuest*'s critical hits are too common, resulting in a high mortality rate among characters: realistic but not much fun. *DragonQuest* combined this with an action-point system, in the first edition at least, so that each action performed costs a few points and a character can continue moving and attacking until its points for that turn run out. Some other role-playing games use this system: *Snapshot*, for example, a *Traveller* combat system.

Hit location is a more popular addition to combat systems; it does away with the D&D situation whereby severely wounded characters fight on as if undamaged until they breathe their last. *RuneQuest* uses this system 'straight', dividing the body into two legs, two arms, head, body and abdomen, which take damage separately. *RuneQuest* combat uses percentages throughout, and is seen as more realistic, but it can be fairly lengthy to play out. *Boot Hill* and *Top Secret* both have hit location, but damage is subtracted from a central fund of hit points. A hit on the right arm will affect the character's shooting, and so on (if he is right-handed). In practice, combat in these two games is lethal for nearly all those involved. The best combat systems, generally, are those that are quick-moving and fun but have an unrealistically low death toll among the characters.

Magic is a basic feature of all Fantasy role-playing. In D&D wizards memorize spells from their books but can store only a limited number, depending on their level, in their memories. When the spell has been cast the Magic-user forgets about it and must re-learn it before using it again. Similarly, spells written on scrolls can be used only once, since the writing fades on reading, and magic wands and staves have a set number of charges which, when expended, must be replaced. This system has been criticized as being illogical and even unrealistic. It may seem inappropriate to talk about 'realism' in a fantasy magic system which has no basis in fact, but it is reasonable to suggest that, if magic existed, it would be more likely to operate in certain ways than in others. Among other Fantasy role-playing games the most common alternative is a power point system whereby each spell a Mage casts costs him a number of power points. When these points run out he can cast no more spells until they regenerate.

Perhaps more realistic yet is a system allowing for spell failure and backfire, often called the Klutz System. Each spell has a chance of failure and every time it is cast this chance increases. If the casting attempt fails by a large margin, the spell will backfire on the Magic-user with unfortunate results. This system has the advantage that, unlike in D&D, extremely powerful spells are available to low-level Magic-users, but at great risk. These systems, or a combination of the two, as seen in *DragonQuest*, can readily be adapted for D&D.

The final major feature common to all role-playing games is an objective. In D&D, experience points are the focus of advance, and when characters hit the 'magic number' they are admitted to a new circle of power, can call themselves less irritating level names, and gain other benefits. Other role-playing games have tried to get away from this syndrome and have largely failed. *Traveller* has no experience point system at all, which can make for an aimless game. *Chivalry and Sorcery* has levels with a difference: training during 'off-hours' adds points automatically. *RuneQuest*, *DragonQuest* and *Top Secret* all have experience-increasing skills, although in the last two it can also be used to increase characteristics. In *Tunnels and Trolls* and *Boot Hill* experience adds solely to characteristics, which improve beyond their initial values, sometimes to disproportionately high levels. *En Garde!*, yet again, escapes the influence of D&D. Although it too has levels, these reflect social standing rather than prowess.

Of all these role-playing games only two can satisfactorily be played solo: *Tunnels and Trolls* and *En Garde!*, the latter because it has no referee anyway, and the former because its simple nature lends itself to the paragraph format of solo dungeons. There exist, moreover, a number of excellent solo scenarios for *Tunnels and Trolls*.

These role-playing games apart, there are some more conventional boardgames that are connected with D&D, mainly growing out of the boom in Fantasy and Science Fiction gaming which was ushered in by D&D's success. *The Sorcerer's Cave* (Ariel Games) is probably most directly related in scenario, although the game mechanics are very different. The idea behind the game is that a sorcerer has hidden his treasure in 'an ever-changing cave of many tunnels and chambers', with monsters and traps to defend it. The practical upshot of this is that the game takes place in a network of underground chambers connected by passages, in which players may find treasure, monsters or both, so that there is little difference from a dungeon.

The game mechanics do without any form of referee. There is a deck of large cards, about fifteen by ten centimetres, on each of which is drawn tunnels or rooms with either an exit or a dead-end in the middle of each edge. As a result the cards will fit together in any combination to produce a map with no loose ends apart from the occasional 'air-bubble' where two dead-ends fit together. As the piece representing the party of adventurers is moved through a selected exit, the top card is taken from the deck and placed in the space adjoining that exit.

Monsters are found in the chambers, which comprise about a third of the deck, and there is a fairly good selection of these creatures, including a gorgon, some spectres, ghouls, dragons, a unicorn and ogres and trolls: the usual jumble, in other words. The treasure guarded by these is either silver, gold, gems, a treasure chest or one of a variety of magic items, all quite nicely thought out and none so strong as to unbalance the game, which is not always the case in D&D. There are also some miscellaneous hazards, such as earthquakes, mutinies and traps, which, by the nature of the system, occur only in rooms.

Simple as the system is, it has rules to cover many concepts familiar to D&D players, such as surprise, charisma and secret doors (of a sort). Combat is simple: either you're killed or you're not as there are no hit points, nor does it hold up play unnecessarily. All in all, the game is fun to play and might serve to introduce members of the family to Dungeons and Dragons proper, but has little to offer in its own right.

After the success of *Sorcerer's Cave*, Ariel produced *Mystic Wood* with a similar game system. It transfers the *Sorcerer's Cave* format to 'an ever-changing forest . . . somewhere between Earth and Heaven'. The setting is drawn from a variety of sources, albeit thankfully consistent ones, including *The Faerie Queen* and *Orlando Furioso*. The wood is a set rectangle, five cards by nine cards, which prevents it sprawling as badly as did *Cave*. The earlier game originally had sixty cards but supplements expanded this number to 150. *Mystic Wood* has forty-five. (It is no cheaper, incidentally, despite the lower number of components: a misprint in the Games Workshop catalogue mentions 'paying aids', and anyone wanting to buy all these games would certainly need them.)

Mystic Wood's design as a whole is tighter than *Cave*'s; each player has a clearly defined objective, rather than the somewhat nebulous search for points in the earlier game. Each player's Knight has a different objective, too, and different strengths and weaknesses, so that some element of role-playing is introduced. All the players have roughly equal chances of winning, it seems, with the possible exception of Guyon. There are enough 'wild cards' in the game (the various 'Mystic' occurrences, for example) to prevent it from becoming static, and the artwork is extremely good, apart from the box cover. This last could be a powerful disincentive to getting the game, but you could do much worse if you want a family game on a Fantasy theme. It is not as simple a game as it looks, either.

One of the few games to dwell on combat underground was Task Force Games' *Valkenberg Castle*, where orcs and humans, arranged in small squads, battle it out in five levels of castle. The magic mechanics are uninspired; the rules for finding treasure and using it are flimsy, and, to be honest, the system of incorporating modern soldiers with grenades and machine-guns is out of place, but the combat rules emphasize the problems of subterranean fighting by having tables based on frontage. In a narrow corridor, a handful of orcs can hold up a human squad for a long time, whereas in a room they can quickly be outflanked.

From the publishers of *RuneQuest*, the Chaosium, there are two boardgames derived from literary sources; *Elric*, being based on Michael Moorcock's *Elric* books (see the Bibliography), and *King Arthur's Knights*, based on the Arthurian legend, as detailed by Malory, Oman, Geoffrey of Monmouth and so on. Both have excellent full-colour glossy maps, probably the best of any of these games, and very good artwork, which, while it would not excuse bad games, goes some way towards enhancing ones with marked strengths and weaknesses.

Elric's main strength lies in the Battalia sheets, which are used to hold armies, thus stopping them from cluttering up the mapboard. As well as the spells held by magicians, the spell cards double as a means of gaining allies. The problem is that of most 'games of the book': namely that the simulation is at times shaky. The system is simple enough, however, to make it possible to bolt on additional rules to cover any particularly weak areas; the way, for example, in which countries end up on the wrong sides could be prevented by some alignment rules, comparable to those for spells. Magic works by drawing a card, either by 'discovering' it in the wilderness, by gaining it from the sack of a town or, in the case of Elric, Yrkoon and Theleb K'aarna, by invoking it during combat, after which it can be played for support in battle. In addition, spells have an alignment, either Chaotic, Neutral or Lawful, and each use of a spell tips the Cosmic Balance towards either Law or Chaos, or back towards Neutrality. If the balance tips over one end, the very fabric of the universe breaks down, which has few exciting effects except that Elric can now be killed and reinforcements stop. In the two-player scenario, Theleb K'aarna is actively trying to do this, so that he can kill Elric; it is not as easy as it might be, either. Artwork is curious in the rulebook, adequate on the one-inch counters, good on the Battalia sheets, and, as usual from the Chaosium, excellent on the mapboard. (All these remarks apply to first-edition *Elric*; a second version is in the pipeline and might be worth waiting for.)

King's Arthur's Knights, by contrast, has a good historical 'feel' to it. The mapboard is divided into regions (North Britain, Logres, Wales et al.), each with its own colour, so that an encounter in, for example, North Britain, is likely to be more dangerous than one in

Logres. The system is simplicity itself: a Knight moves, usually, into an adjacent province and picks a card of the appropriate colour. This will give him an encounter with another Knight, a woman or a magician, all of which can be resolved by a single die roll. Combat is simple, the one roll deciding whether the attacker or defender wins, and how many wounds the loser receives; the effect of wounds being that turns are lost while recovering. Encounters with women usually result in the Knight taking an adventure card, this giving the opportunity to do some trivial task for a few points.

The game revolves around the acquisition of Chivalry Points, which can be gained from adventures or defeating Knights (either from cards or other players) in combat. To win, a Knight needs a certain total of chivalry points, and treasure to go with it, the precise figures in each case depending on whether the Knight is a Knight-Errant, a Knight-at-Arms or a Great Knight.

Apart from the basic rules, there are opportunities to go on a quest for some magic item, such as the Holy Grail, Gwenbaus' Book or Solomon's Boat. There are also opportunities to back out of quests, which is useful if you have been told to hunt the Shroud of Turin, which does not exist in the game. The various questing objects are represented by yellow cards distributed randomly throughout the map, each with a random guardian, usually one which has to be overcome in normal or magical combat, but occasionally something special, such as the infuriating 'riddling dwarf'. The treasures and guardians are kept face down, but players sometimes get a chance to see one of them after magical combat, so that the quest becomes akin to a game of pelmanism as you try to remember whether the magic chess set is in Tintagel or Wandesborow.

Special rules also deal with such things as road and sea movement, madness, becoming a hermit, poison wounds and wandering holy people, and allow Knights to buy castles or even to marry. The map is a wonderfully colourful one of Britain as was, and all the other components are attractive, with the exception of the Knight counters, which are best done away with and replaced with Britains' models. Considering how much goes on in it, the game is easy and quick to play, and compelling until the attraction wears off. It is also quite simple to explain to anyone wanting to join in, which is another bonus.

The Chaosium also produce *Dragon Pass*, originally *White Bear and Red Moon*, from which *RuneQuest*'s world is derived. It is essentially a straightforward two-player board wargame with a Fantasy setting. One player commands the moon-worshipping Lunar Empire, which dominates the world of Glorantha. Just outside the Empire is the country of Sartar, which is controlled by the second player. The map shows Dragon Pass, which includes Sartar and the furthest extent of the Lunar Empire, along with a number of independent territories between the two. Each side has a regular army of both soldiers and magicians but also has a number of units with special powers. These include superheroes, persons each with the power of hundreds, and exotic units such as the Lunar Empire's Crimson Bat, which at certain phases of the moon must devour soldiers, or Sartar's wasps, which cause confusion and disruption. Combat is divided into three main sections: magical, missile and melee. There are three types of magic: spiritual, physical and exotic, but there is the additional feature that the Lunar magical power varies with the different phases of the moon. In addition to their own armies, players try to obtain allies from the independent tribes and individuals who populate Dragon Pass. Although it takes longer to play than the other family type games mentioned before, it is extremely enjoyable, its appeal owing more than a little to the well-detailed descriptions of the inhabitants of the world and their interesting history.

Another Fantasy boardgame, whose success derives from similar features, is T.S.R.'s *Divine Right*. The feel of the game is much the same as that of *Dragon Pass* but any number up to six can play. Their countries, however, have either military or magical might, but not both. One nation alone, 'The Black Hand', has both, and hence is the strongest. Each player is represented on the board by their monarch counter which, if killed, puts the player out of the game. Here, too, winning revolves around securing non-player allies, but alliances can be broken by other players, which is not so in *Dragon Pass*. It is, unfortunately, too simple to appeal to veteran wargamers, while perhaps too complicated for the whole family.

S.P.I. publish *War of the Ring*, the game of the book. As the game is licensed by Tolkien Enterprises, it can call a Hobbit a Hobbit without fear of retribution, and it has as far as possible the accuracy that might be expected from S.P.I., who are best known as manufacturers of historically based games. All the major characters from the trilogy are included, both as counters and as cards, with an illustration on one side and attributes on the other, with the exception of Tom Bombadil, who also was left out of Ralph Bakshi's film and the B.B.C. radio adaptation (such is life). The game comes in three versions: a 'character game', which is hardly worth playing; an 'army game', with all the military units from the trilogy, as well as the characters, which is well worth playing; and a three-player game, which incorporates Saruman as a third player rather than as a minion of Sauron. More realistic, it might be argued, but the White Wizard has little chance of winning unless the other two players all but forget his existence (which, to be fair, has been known).

In the Standard game, the Fellowship can win in one of two ways: by dropping the ring into the Cracks of Doom or by capturing vast areas of the mapboard, including Isengard and Barad-dur; if the Fellowship player can achieve this, he or she can probably get the ring to Orodruin anyway. The Dark Power player can win by capturing the ring (which can happen if the ringbearer uses it too often and turns into a ringwraith), or by capturing various areas. This latter method is more feasible for Sauron than for the Fellowship, as Mordor has practically unlimited armies when it mobilizes, both of orcs and southern men, haradrim, and even oliphaunts. The Dark Power player has a hard time making use of his forces, though, because of the 'shadow point' system. Each time Sauron performs any action he has to pay a 'shadow point', of which he has somewhere between eight and thirteen each move. This limits the effectiveness of Mordor's armies, whereas the less centralized Fellowship does not suffer from this problem.

Some of the other mechanisms used are less successful; the search rules, for example, and in early copies of the game Frodo and Gandalf are instantly recognizable because of the green stripe on the backs of their counters, or the individual combat system, where characters queue up to fight. Many of the good design features reappear in *Freedom in the Galaxy*, a game of galactic rebellion à la *Star Wars*, and infinitely superior to any one of the games bearing that name.

Another game of the book is Avalon Hill's *Dune*, based on the books of the same name by Frank Herbert. The game itself was designed by Eon Products and has elements of both Fantasy and role-playing, although it is, in essence, a fairly simple boardgame.

The game can accommodate between two and six players, but in practice the more the merrier. Each becomes the leader of one of the six factions vying for power on the planet Dune: Atreides, Harkonnen, Bene Gesserit, Guild, Imperial and Fremen. Each character has his or her own special powers, such as the Bene Gesserit *Voice* or the Atreides' *Prescience*. The game system is based on *Cosmic Encounter* from Eon Products, a simpler game which all the family can play.

It should be borne in mind that, with over fifty role-playing systems currently on the market and more planned for release, we cannot hope to mention all of them, only those which we have played. Indeed, whole books have been written on role-playing, most of them by psychologists, and this one chapter cannot rival these. To those whose systems have been passed over, we apologize.

One game, finally, deserves mention as having a system totally divorced from that of any other role-playing game. In *Killer* (Steve Jackson Games) players *are* their characters, and the game takes place in real-time, often over a period of days. The players try to 'kill' each other with guns (water pistols, dart guns, even bananas), bombs (drawing pins and balloons, alarm clocks), poison or electricity (both non-lethal to the actual player). The rules divide weapons into classes: A (completely safe), B, C and D (actually lethal). The game is probably at its best if mainly class A weapons are used, with a few from class B. (The rules suggest that the use of rubber spiders as tarantulas may give some players heart attacks, but you could probably risk it.) If handguns are legal, the game tends to degenerate to a situation where a handful of psychos with water pistols wipe each other out, causing a good deal of mess and annoyance to players and innocent bystanders.

Killer, however, depends on what you put into it. At its best, with a variety of subtle and ingenious bombs in use, along with poisons of various sorts, not just the over-used contact poison, it induces a sense of collective paranoia that is marvellous to behold. It is also as close to true role-playing as a game can get without being life itself.

List of model manufacturers

✠   ✠

(The products of American manufacturers are usually distributed by games shops or distributers in the U.K.)

Ariel/Philmar (*The Sorcerer's Cave, Mystic Wood*): 47–53 Dace Road, London E3 2NG.

Asgard Miniatures (figures): 36 High Pavement, Nottingham NG1 1MN.

Avalon Hill (*Dune* and other boardgames): 4517 Harford Road, Baltimore, Maryland 2124, U.S.A. (U.K. distributor: Avalon Hill Games, 650 High Road, London N12.

The ChaoSium (*RuneQuest, Elric, King Arthur's Knights*): PO Box 6302, Albany, California 94706, U.S.A.

Chronicle Miniatures (figures): Unit 14, Engineer Park, Sandycroft, Clwyd.

Citadel Miniatures (figures; U.K. distributer for Ral Partha): 10 Victoria Street, Newark, Notts.

Citadel Miniatures U.S. Inc.: PO Box 12352, Cincinnati, Ohio 45212, U.S.A.

Eon Products, Inc. (*Cosmic Encounter*, Quirks): 96 Stockton Street, Dorchester, Massachusetts 02124, U.S.A.

Esdevium Games (major mail-order suppliers): 185 Victoria Road, Aldershot, Hants GU11 1J.

Fantasy Games Unlimited Inc. (*Chivalry and Sorcery, Space Opera, Bushido* et al.): 240 Mineola Boulevard, Mineola, New York State 11501, U.S.A.

Flying Buffalo (*Tunnels and Trolls*): PO Box 1467, Scottsdale, Arizona 85252, U.S.A.

Flying Buffalo: Bath Street, Walsall, West Midlands.

Game Designers' Workshop (*Traveller, En Garde!*): 203 North Street, Normal, Illinois 61761, U.S.A.

Games Centre (major games shop): 22 Oxford Street, London W1

Games of Liverpool (major games shop, mail-order supplier; distributer for F.G.U.I.): 50–54 Manchester Street, Liverpool L1 6ER.

Games Workshop (major games shop, mail-order supplier; publisher of *White Dwarf*; distributer for the ChaoSium, G. D. W., Eon and their own games): 27–29 Sunbeam Road, London NW10 6JP.

Judges Guild (modules, accessories): RR 8, Box 9, 1221 North Sunnyside Road, Decatur, Illinois 62522, U.S.A.

Metagaming (*Melee, Wizard* and *The Fantasy Trip*): PO Box 15346, Austin, Texas 78761, U.S.A.

Ral Partha (figures): PO Box 9116, Cincinnati, Ohio 45209, U.S.A.

Simulations Publications Incorporated (S.P.I.) (*DragonQuest, War of the Ring, Ares*): 257 Park Avenue South, New York, New York State 10010, U.S.A. (NOTE THAT S.P.I HAVE RECENTLY BEEN TAKEN OVER BY T.S.R.)

Simpubs Ltd: Freepost, Oakfield House, 60 Oakfield Road, Altrincham, Cheshire WA15 8EW.

Standard Games and Publications Ltd (cardboard figures): Arlon House, Station Road, Kings Langley, Herts.

Steve Jackson Games (*Killer*, cardboard figures): PO Box 15346, Austin, Texas 78761, U.S.A.

Tactical Studies Rules Hobbies, Inc. (T.S.R.) (*D & D, Boot Hill, Gamma World, Top Secret*, etc.): PO Box 756, Lake Geneva, Wisconsin 53147, U.S.A.

T.S.R. Hobbies (U.K.) Ltd: The Mill, Rathmore Road, Cambridge CB1 4AD.

Task Force Games (*Valkenberg Castle*): 405 South Crockett, Amarillo, Texas 79104, U.S.A.

All these addresses are, to the best of our knowledge, correct at the time of writing.

✠ Bibliography ✠

One of the best sources of ideas for D&D is Fantasy literature. Obviously, any list of this sort must be subjective, but all the authors listed here should prove useful for D.M.s and enjoyable for players.

(1) Writers most or all of whose works are relevant to D&D
(The books listed are illustrative of the authors' work, and are not necessarily the first in a series.)

Asprin, Bob, *Another Fine Myth, Myth Conceptions, Thieves' World* (ed.), *Tales from the Vulgar Unicorn* (ed.).

Bradley, Marion Zimmer, *Darkover Landfall, The Heritage of Hastur,* etc.

Burroughs, Edgar Rice, *A Princess of Mars, At the Earth's Core, The Land That Time Forgot,* etc.

Cabell, James Branch, *Figures of Earth, Biography of the Life of Manuel,* etc.

Carter, Lin, *The Warrior of World's End, The Wizard of Lemuria, Jandar of Callisto,* and some *Conan* stories (see Howard).

Davidson, Aram, *The Phoenix and the Mirror, The Island under the Earth.*

De Camp, L. Sprague, *The Tower of Zanid, The Tritonian Ring, The Fallible Fiend,* etc.
   with Pratt, Fletcher, *The Incompleat Enchanter,* etc.

Donaldson, Stephen, *Lord Foul's Bane, The Illearth War,* etc.

Dunsany, Lord, *The King of Elfland's Daughter, The Sword of Welleran,* etc.

Eddison, E. R., *The Worm Ouroboros.*

Farmer, Philip José, *To Your Scattered Bodies Go, The Maker of Universes,* etc.

Herbert, Frank, *Dune,* etc.

Howard, Robert E., *The Coming of Conan, Conan of Cimmeria,* etc. (series added to by L. Sprague de Camp and Lin Carter, q.v.).

Lee, Tanith, *The Birthgrave, Companions on the Road.*

Le Guin, Ursula K., *The Wizard of Earthsea, The Left Hand of Darkness, The Word for World is Forest,* etc.

Leiber, Fritz, *Swords and Deviltry, The Big Time*, etc.
Lewis, C. S., *The Lion, the Witch and the Wardrobe, Out of the Silent Planet*, etc.
Lovecraft, H. P., *The Shadow over Innsmouth, The Case of Charles Dexter Ward*, etc.
McCaffrey, Anne, *Dragonflight*, etc.
MacDonald, George, *Lilith, The Princess and the Goblin*.
McIntyre, Vonda, *Dreamsnake, The Exile Waiting*.
McKillip, Patricia, *The Riddle-Master of Hed*, etc.
Merritt, A., *The Dwellers in the Mirage*, etc.
Moorcock, Michael, *The Eternal Champion, Elric of Melniboné, The Knight of the Swords, The Jewel in the Skull, An Alien Heat*, etc.
Norton, André, *The Year of the Unicorn, Web of the Witch World*, etc.
Tolkien, J. R. R., *The Hobbit, The Lord of the Rings*, etc.
Vance, Jack, *Dying Earth, The Dragon Masters, City of the Csasch, The Star King*.
White, T. H., *The Once and Future King, The Book of Merlyn*.
Zelazny, Roger, *The Doors of His Face, the Lamps of His Mouth and Other Stories, Nine Princes in Amber*, etc.

*(2) Writers in other genres, mainly Science Fiction and minor Fantasy writers
(Titles are given only where necessary.)*

Douglas Adams
Brian Aldiss
Poul Anderson (*War of the Wing-Men*)
Piers Anthony
Isaac Asimov
J. G. Ballard
Beowulf
Alfred Bester
James Blish (the 'After Such Knowledge' trilogy)
Jorge Luis Borges
Pierre Boulle
Ben Bova
Leigh Brackett
Ray Bradbury
John Brunner
Thomas Bullfinch (*Mythology*)
Michael Butterworth
J. W. Campbell
Lewis Carroll
Geoffrey Chaucer
C. J. Cherryh
John Christopher
Arthur C. Clarke
Stanton A. Coblentz
Dante
Samuel R. Delany
Philip K. Dick
Peter Dickinson
Sir Arthur Conan Doyle
Epic of Gilgamesh
Alan Garner
Robert Graves
H. Rider Haggard
Harry Harrison

M. John Harrison (*The Pastel City*)
Harvard Lampoon (*Bored of the Rings*)
Robert E. Heinlein (*Glory Road*)
Herodotus
Homer
Ted Hughes
John Jakes
Charles Kingsley (*The Heroes*)
Nigel Kneale
Katherine Kurtz
Andrew Lang (*In the Wrong Paradise and Other Stories*)
Lucian
Julian May (*The Saga of the Exiles*)
Sir Thomas More
Larry Niven and Jerry Pournelle
John Norman
Andrew J. Offutt
Ovid
Plato
Mack Reynolds
Fred Saberhagen
William Shakespeare
Robert Shea and Robert Anton Wilson
Robert Silverberg (*Lord Valentine's Castle*)
Clifford D. Simak
Sir Gawain and the Green Knight
Clark Ashton Smith
Norman Spinrad
Christopher Stasheff
Arkady and Boris Strugatsky
Jonathon Swift
A. E. Van Vogt
Virgil
Chelsea Quinn Yarbro

(3) Non-fiction works relevant to D&D

There are, at the moment, rather few books specifically about the game. Two are: *Fantasy Role-Playing Games*, by J. E. Holmes, published by Arms and Armour Press, and *Fantasy Wargaming*, by Bruce Galloway (Patrick Stephens Ltd). Any history books about the medieval period (those by W. L. Warren, for example) can give insights into the kind of society that D&D uses, as can books about ancient wargames relevant to pitched battles, which sometimes occur in D&D. One other book that deserves mention is *The Warlock of Firetop Mountain*, by Steve Jackson and Ian Livingstone (Puffin Books), which is intended to act as an introduction to role-playing without the complexity of the larger games.

✠ Glossary ✠

D&D uses many words as a specialist vocabulary, some of them not occurring in normal English and many being used in a sense different from normal. This glossary defines the most common usages.

Ability	(1) Synonymous with **Attribute**. (2) Used of skills associated with a particular character class, such as **Clerical Turning** of **Undead** or **Thieves'** lock-picking.
Adventure	The actions taken by the **characters** and the events which happen to them between setting out on an expedition and returning from it.
Adventurer	A **player character** or a **retainer**.
Alignment	A capsule description of a **character's** behaviour in terms of **Law**, **Neutrality** and **Chaos**.
Animal	A non-Fantastical **monster**, generally of low intelligence. A Mule or a Giant Beetle, for example.
Armour class	A number representing a **character's** or a **monster's** relative protection from harm, including physical armour, magical bonuses and dexterity. Low numbers indicate better protection than high ones.
Artefact	A manufactured item, especially a magical one.
Attribute	A **character's** six attributes define his physical and mental 'make-up'. Each is on a separate scale from 3 to 18. See also **Strength**, **Intelligence**, **Wisdom**, **Dexterity**, **Constitution** and **Charisma**.
Background	Information about events which have occurred before the start of the **adventure**.
Caller	Used of the player (and, to a lesser extent, of his **character**) who is nominally in charge of the **party** and acts as its spokesman.
Campaign	A series of **adventures** taking place in the same world or **setting**. Also used of the playing **sessions** in which these **adventures** are played out.

Chaotic	One of the three **alignments**, which values randomness and individuality against **Law**.
Character (player)	A persona generated by a player and controlled by him during the game.
Character generation	The process of determining a **character's** characteristics. Discussed at length in Chapter 2.
Characteristic	A facet of a **character's** composition. Includes **attributes**, height, weight and **alignment**.
Character sheet	A piece of paper on which are recorded details of a **character's characteristics, equipment** and experience.
Charisma	One of the six **attributes**. It quantifies its **character's** personal charm to members of its own **race**.
Cleric	One of the four basic character classes. A man-of-God, with some fighting ability and a few **spells**, mostly to do with healing.
Common	A simple language, conveniently assumed to be spoken by all **characters** and many **monsters**.
Constitution	One of the six **attributes**. It quantifies its **character's** physical build and capacity to withstand **damage**.
Copper piece	A unit of **money**, worth 1/100th of a **gold piece**.
Damage	Physical harm done to a **character** or **monster**, usually in combat. The amount of **damage** is the amount subtracted from **hit points**.
Demi-Human	A **humanoid** creature, which is one of the permitted **character races**, other than **human**. Dwarves, Elves and **Halflings** are the **demi-Humans** in Basic D&D.
Dexterity	One of the six **attributes**. It quantifies a **character's** agility, speed and co-ordination.
Dungeon	The generic name for any area where an **adventure** takes place, except a town or wilderness. Usually underground.
Dungeon Master (D. M.)	The gamer who runs play, interpreting the rules, designing the **dungeons** and acting for **monsters** and **non-player characters**.
Dwarf	One of the four **character races**. A short, stocky bearded **demi-Human**.
Electrum piece	A unit of **money**, worth half a **gold piece**.
Elf	One of the four **character races**. A slender, graceful **demi-Human**.
Encounter	A meeting between the **party** and **monsters** or **non-player characters**.

Encumbrance	The weight and burden of the **equipment** and **treasure** carried by a **character**.
Equipment	**Artefacts** and other items carried by a **character** on an **adventure**.
Experience level	A quantification of a **character**'s relative powers and abilities. On a scale of 1 upwards.
Experience points	Often abbreviated to XP. Rewards given to **characters** for actions performed on **adventures**. A set number is needed to reach a given **experience level**.
Fantasy	A genre of stories and games set in a world different from our own. Includes **Science Fiction**, although Fantasy worlds are usually taken to have a quasi-medieval **setting**.
Fanzine	An abbreviation of 'fan magazine'. A magazine dealing with D&D, **role-playing** games in general, or with **Science Fiction**.
Fighter	One of the four basic **character** classes. The fighter is primarily concerned with physical combat.
Figures	Small scale models of **characters**, **monsters** and **artefacts**. Commercially available ones are typically unpainted, metal and on a scale of 25mm = 6 feet. Discussed at greater length in Chapter 6.
'Freeze-frame'	A type of **dungeon** room in which actions are in the process of being performed by the inmates when the **party** enters, regardless of when this entrance occurs on an absolute scale.
Games convention	Often abbreviated to Con. A public meeting, typically attended by upwards of a hundred people, where games are played and manufacturers display their wares.
Giant class	A **humanoid monster** which is not **Human** or demi-Human. The class includes goblins, ogres, bugbears and the like.
Gold piece	The basic unit of **money**. Worth very roughly £10 in today's money.
Group	Synonymous with **party**. Also used of the players and D.M. together.
'Hack-and-Slay'	A style of play which emphasizes combat rather than problem-solving.
Halfling	A short **demi-Human** with hairy legs and feet. One of the four standard character races.

Henchman	An ordinary, non-specialized **Human** or demi-**Human** hired by a **party** or **character** to aid on an **adventure**.
Hireling	An expert hired by a **character** to perform some specialized task. A blacksmith or a cobbler, for example.
Hit dice	The number of d8s rolled to determine a **monster's hit points**. Hence used as a convenient assessment of a monster's relative deadliness.
Hit points	The amount of **damage** that a **character** or **monster** can sustain before it dies.
Holy water	Water which has been blessed or otherwise rendered holy. Causes **damage** to **Undead** creatures.
Human	One of the four standard **character** races.
Humanoid	A creature with roughly **Human** shape, but not necessarily size. Usually bipedal and with two arms.
Infravision	The ability to see into the infra-red part of the spectrum and thus 'see in the dark' by sensing heat.
Initiative	In an **encounter**, the side with initiative has first choice of action. Initiative is determined by a die roll.
Intelligence	One of the six **attributes**. It quantifies memory, I.Q., retentive memory and **spell**-casting ability.
Key (Dungeon)	A list of the contents of a **dungeon**, together with some means of determining their location on the **dungeon** map.
Lawful	A type of **alignment** which values order and organization above **chaos**.
Level	Used of a variety of things (e.g. **spell** level, **dungeon** level, **experience** level) to denote relative power or danger. Lower numbers indicate less advanced levels.
Lycanthrope	A were-creature.
Magic item	An **artefact** whose normal effects have been altered by magical means. Magic swords, magic armour, wands, amulets and scrolls are all examples of magic items.
Magic-user	One of the four basic **character** classes. A Magic-user will use **spells** rather than engaging in physical combat.
Mapper	The player who makes a rough map of the **dungeon** as it is traversed. Also used of his **character**.
Marching order	The order in which **characters** are travelling.
Melee	Hand-to-hand combat, where the participants are separated by a distance of 5 feet or less.
Melee round	The basic unit of time in **melee**. Represents a time of 10 seconds.

Miniatures	Synonymous with **figures**.
Mini-module	A small **module**, typically playable in one **session**.
Missile	Any object or **weapon** capable of inflicting **damage** at a distance of more than 5 feet.
Module	A pre-packaged **adventure**. Usually commercial.
Money	A coin-type medium of exchange, acceptable by most shopkeepers and other traders. In D&D, curiously enough, all coins are of the same size and weight (1/10 of a pound), which implies that those made of the denser metals must be hollow. Coin types are **copper piece**, **electrum piece**, **gold piece**, **platinum piece** and **silver piece**.
Monster	Any non-**Human** creature; also used of any non-**humanoid** creature.
'Monty Hall' or 'Monty Haul'	A type of **dungeon** or **campaign** where rewards are disproportionately large when compared to dangers faced by the **party**. So called after a TV personality who hosted a quiz show with similar characteristics.
Morale check	**Monsters** or **non-player characters** who are in danger must undergo a morale check to determine whether they flee. Further discussed in Chapter 5.
Name level	The **level** of **experience** at which a **character** class **level** name becomes the same from that **level** upwards.
Natural roll	The number which appears when a die is rolled before any modifications are made to it.
Neutral	A type of **alignment** which values self-interest above **Law** or **Chaos**.
Non-player character	Usually abbreviated to N.P.C. Any **character** controlled not by **players**, but by the **D.M.**
Paralysis	Loss of motor function of nerves. A consequence of being hit by certain types of **monster**, Carrion Crawlers, for example.
Party	A number of **adventurers** in co-operation with each other. Synonymous with one meaning of **group**.
Petrifaction	Turning to stone. A consequence of being attacked by certain types of **monster**, medusae, for example.
Platinum piece	A unit of **money**, worth 5 gold pieces.
'Pocket universe'	A small area, created by the **D.M.** to test out prospective innovations to the game.
Poison	A substance intended to cause **damage** or death by interference with the body's metabolism.

Polyhedral dice	Random number generators, usually in the form of Platonic solids with numbers on the faces. Designated d4, d6, d8, d12 and d20.
Polymorph	To change the shape of something by magical means.
Prime requisite	The **attribute** which is most important for a given **character** class.
Race	The species of a **player-character**. See **Human, Dwarf, Elf** and **Halfling**.
Referee	Synonymous with **D.M.**; or his equivalent in a different game.
Retainer	A person hired by a **character** or **party** to help on an **adventure**. See **henchman, hireling**.
Role-playing	The assumption of a persona not one's own.
Round	Synonymous with **melee round**.
Saving throw/ Saving roll	The number which must be thrown (or higher) to avoid some adverse consequence.
Scenario	A **module** or **mini-module**. Also used synonymously with **setting**.
Science Fiction	A type of **Fantasy**, set in the future or far future, or with some plausible-seeming rationale or technology.
Session	A time spent playing D&D, running continuously. Typically an afternoon; rarely longer than a weekend.
Setting	The background for an **adventure** or **campaign**. Includes some details of social mores, technology, political systems and so on.
Silver piece	A unit of **money**, worth 1/10 of a **gold piece**.
Spell	A magical incantation with the purpose (and usually the effect) of bringing about an alteration in reality. Used by **Magic-users** and **Clerics**.
Strength	One of the six **attributes**. It quantifies power and muscular force.
Surprise	One side in an **encounter** being caught unprepared. The other side receives a free **round** of activity.
Thief	One of the four basic **character** classes. Concerned with the arts of deception, guile, trickery and stealth.
To hit roll, the	The least number which must be rolled to cause **damage** in combat.
Trap	An **artefact** or construction intended to cause injury, death or otherwise act against the interests of anyone encountering it.
Treasure	**Money**, gems and **magic items** and other **artefacts** discovered in an **adventure**.

Tribal	A type of **monster** which lives in tribes. Used especially of Goblins, Orcs and the smaller **Giant class monsters.**
Trick	A type of **trap** involving **non-playing characters** and **monsters.**
Turn	The standard unit of time in D&D. Represents 10 minutes – of **character** (not player) time.
Turn (Undead)	A **Cleric's ability** to cause **Undead** to flee from him.
Undead	A class of **monster** typically once dead and now reanimated. Includes Skeletons, Zombies, Ghouls, etc.
Wandering monster	A **monster** not plotted on the **dungeon key,** but whose appearance is rolled randomly.
Weapon	An **artefact** used to cause **damage** to a **character** or **monster.** See also **magic item.**
Wisdom	One of the six **attributes.** It quantifies mental stability, faith and common-sense.

Authors' note

We owe a few apologies to our readership. The first is to do with prices, which are hardly ever quoted in money but nearly always in terms of the cost of the Basic Rulebook. This is not as useful as it might be, but we consider that it is better to quote relative prices than to give actual figures which will have become obsolete by the time this book reaches you. Actual prices can be found in current issues of magazines or catalogues.

The second is made necessary by the book's multiple authorship. Rather than write every word by committee, we have split the book up into sections, each with a specialized author. This means that there will be different styles at different points in the book; if this jars, we apologize. It may have led to a certain degree of unconscious repetition, but it is better, we feel, to repeat where relevant than to leave something unsaid. It should be emphasized, however, that we have all read, and stand by, every word of the book as a whole.

The book is aimed at a wide spectrum of readers, and at various different levels. Some parts of it may therefore, seem patronizing to the experienced, or confusing to the novice. We hope, even so, that everyone will find something of interest in the book, and will forgive us the parts that are less relevant to them.

One major problem has been that of knowing, always, where our ideas have come from. While we have never consciously lifted any part of this book, we have all read widely in magazines and books about Dungeons and Dragons and other role-playing games. If anything has been 'stolen' we apologize sincerely, but it should be remembered, especially with regard to Chapter Nine, that if two reviews of a game differ completely, one or both of them must be incorrect.

One final apology is due – to our female readership. We have usually used 'he' and 'his', both because 'he or she' is clumsy and because the majority of Dungeons and Dragons players are male. We are aware that our solution is not totally satisfactory, and that the use of a female wizard is a token gesture and rather stereotyped to boot, but we claim that in this instance the fault lies with the English language and not with us.

Acknowledgements

Our thanks are due to everyone who has, wittingly or unwittingly, contributed to the writing of this book. This includes, especially, Andy Slack and Captain Flint, with both of whom we had useful discussions, in some cases before we started writing or knew we were going to; those of our friends who helped (and some who didn't); in particular everyone we've ever played D&D with, all the Strat. Soc. regulars, those whose characters were in some way appropriated (Angus 'Slammer', 'Zhod' Toby, Marcus 'Hotfa' and Colette — a different one); everyone at Penguin; our long-suffering parents for all their help and encouragement; Mr Hammond for getting the whole thing off the ground and helping to keep it airborne; finally, to Gary Gygax and Dave Arneson, who invented D&D and without whom none of this would have been possible.

✠ Index ✠

MORE ABOUT PENGUINS
AND PELICANS

For further information about books available from Penguins please write to Dept EP, Penguin Books Ltd, Harmondsworth, Middlesex UB7 0DA.

In the U.S.A.: For a complete list of books available from Penguins in the United States write to Dept CS, Penguin Books, 625 Madison Avenue, New York, New York 10022.

In Canada: For a complete list of books available from Penguins in Canada write to Penguin Books Canada Ltd, 2801 John Street, Markham, Ontario L3R 1B4.

In Australia: For a complete list of books available from Penguins in Australia write to the Marketing Department, Penguin Books Australia Ltd, P.O. Box 257, Ringwood, Victoria 3134.

In New Zealand: For a complete list of books available from Penguins in New Zealand write to the Marketing Department, Penguin Books (N.Z.) Ltd, P.O. Box 4019, Auckland 10.

HOW TO WIN AT PAC-MAN

Pac-Man is becoming the world's most popular computer game, outstripping all its rivals, even the invincible Space Invaders. Everybody is playing it! And this colourful, fully illustrated Penguin is the first book to tell you how to win. Using this book as a guideline, you can enhance your own style of Pac-Manship to discover the inexhaustible permutations of the game and the strategies behind the highest scores.

THE PLAYER'S STRATEGY GUIDE TO ATARI® VCS HOME-VIDEO GAMES
Arnie Katz and Bill Kunkel

Here are the playing instructions and winning strategies to ensure success in your battle against the computer, with scoring scales that let you rate *your* skill against the masters.

There are hot tips from ace-player 'Video Frank' and an exclusive complete buyer's guide to every Atari®-compatible cartridge as well as previews of soon-to-be-released games.

THE COMPLETE HANDBOOK OF VIDEO
David Owen and Mark Dunton

Here is everything you need to know about video: how to make the best buy and how to get the most out of it, whether you're using your video in the home or at work. This indispensable handbook gives full, up-to-date information on recorders, television and cameras, plus the latest details on video games, video computers and video security.

Penguins for new dimensions in games and puzzles

NOTES ON RUBIK'S MAGIC CUBE
David Singmaster

So you've solved the Cube . . . now what? How, exactly, does it work? How do you do the duo twist and the mono swap? What is a Cubist's thumb? Singmaster's unique blue guide is specially for everyone who thought they knew everything about the Cube, it's packed with new information, plus the latest news and results from Cubists all over the world.

'The definitive treatise' – Douglas Hofstadter
'Une veritable bible du "cubiste"' – *Science et Vie*
'Beyond all understanding' – *New Standard*

GÖDEL, ESCHER, BACH:
AN ETERNAL GOLDEN BRAID
Douglas R. Hofstadter

Linking the music of J. S. Bach, the graphic art of Escher and the mathematical theorems of Gödel, as well as ideas drawn from logic, biology, psychology, physics and linguistics, Douglas Hofstadter illuminates one of the greatest mysteries of modern science: the nature of human thought processes.

'Extraordinary, exhilarating . . . this splendid *tour de force* . . . leaves you feeling you have had a first-class workout in the best mental gymnasium in town' – *New Statesman*

THE MAGIC OF LEWIS CARROLL
Edited by John Fisher

Behind the seemingly absurd events in Lewis Carroll's fantasies of Alice and the Snark there lie a mass of mathematical games and puzzles, logical conundrums, word-plays and conjuring tricks. Although his serious work as a mathematician at Oxford was unremarkable, Carroll was able to weave webs of improbability in his 'entertainments' which can confuse even the best brains, and have earned him his place in the history of mathematical and logical thought.

In this thoroughly entertaining collection, John Fisher gathers together both Carroll's own puzzles and other contemporary tricks and games which influenced him.